TAKE TIME FOR YOU

Self-Care Action Plans for Educators

TINA H. BOOGREN

Solution Tree | Press
a division of
Solution Tree

555 North Morton Street
Bloomington, IN 47404
800.733.6786 (toll free) / 812.336.7700
FAX: 812.336.7790

email: info@SolutionTree.com
SolutionTree.com

Visit **go.SolutionTree.com/instruction** to download the free reproducibles in this book.

Printed in the United States of America

Library of Congress Cataloging-in-Publication Data

Names: Boogren, Tina, author.
Title: Take time for you : self-care action plans for educators / Tina H.
   Boogren.
Description: Bloomington, IN : Solution Tree Press, [2018] | Includes
   bibliographical references and index.
Identifiers: LCCN 2017049714 | ISBN 9781945349713 (perfect bound)
Subjects: LCSH: Teachers--Psychology. | Teachers--Job satisfaction. |
   Self-help techniques.
Classification: LCC LB2840 .B66 2018 | DDC 371.1--dc23 LC record available at https://lccn.loc
.gov/2017049714

Solution Tree
Jeffrey C. Jones, CEO
Edmund M. Ackerman, President

Solution Tree Press
President and Publisher: Douglas M. Rife
Editorial Director: Sarah Payne-Mills
Art Director: Rian Anderson
Managing Production Editor: Kendra Slayton
Senior Production Editor: Tonya Maddox Cupp
Senior Editor: Amy Rubenstein
Copy Editor: Evie Madsen
Proofreader: Jessi Finn
Text and Cover Designer: Abigail Bowen

ACKNOWLEDGMENTS

This book is for all the amazing educators I've had the pleasure of working with over the years either as colleagues or as participants in my workshops and trainings. Thank you for relentlessly pursuing excellence for the students that you so beautifully serve and for doing the work with grace and determination amid a world that sometimes forgets just how important you are. I will forever be your fiercest advocate.

Solution Tree Press would like to thank the following reviewers:

Pam Ertel
Third-Grade Teacher
Minden Elementary School
Minden, Nevada

Stephanie Gurule-Leyba
Biomedical Sciences Teacher
Capital High School
Santa Fe, New Mexico

Amy Hysick
Science Teacher
Cicero-North Syracuse High School
Cicero, New York

Argine Safari
2017 New Jersey State Teacher
   of the Year
Education Advocate and Clinician
Music Teacher
Pascack Valley High School
Hillsdale, New Jersey

Jason Sickel
Choral Director
Blue Valley North High School
Overland Park, Kansas

Amber Vlasnik
Mathematics Instructional Coach
Lincoln High School
Lincoln, Nebraska

Shelly Vroegh
Fifth-Grade Teacher /
   Instructional Coach
Lakewood Elementary School
Norwalk, Iowa

Visit **go.SolutionTree.com/instruction** to download
the free reproducibles in this book.

TABLE OF CONTENTS

Reproducible pages are in italics.

CHAPTER 3
Safety Needs 43

CHAPTER 4
Belonging Needs 55

CHAPTER 5
Esteem Needs 71

CHAPTER 6
Self-Actualization Needs 87

About the Author

Tina H. Boogren, PhD, is a former classroom teacher, English department chair, teacher mentor, instructional coach, professional developer, athletic coach, and building-level leader. She has presented at the school, district, state, and national levels and was a featured speaker at the International Literacy Association annual conference and Barnes & Noble's educators' nights.

Tina was a 2007 finalist for Colorado Teacher of the Year and received the Douglas County School District Outstanding Teacher Award eight years in a row, from 2002 to 2009. In addition to writing articles for the National Writing Project's *The Voice* and *The Quarterly*, she authored *The Beginning Teacher's Field Guide: Embarking On Your First Years*; *In the First Few Years: Reflections of a Beginning Teacher*; and *Supporting Beginning Teachers*. She coauthored *Motivating and Inspiring Students: Strategies to Awaken the Learner*, and contributed to *Middle School Teaching: A Guide to Methods and Resources* and *Becoming a Reflective Teacher*.

Tina holds a bachelor's degree from the University of Iowa, a master's degree with an administrative endorsement from the University of Colorado Denver, and a doctorate in educational administration and policy studies from the University of Denver. She is currently pursuing a master of fine arts degree from Regis University.

To learn more about Tina's work, visit www.facebook.com/selfcareforeducators or follow @THBoogren on Twitter and Instagram.

To book Tina H. Boogren for professional development, contact pd@SolutionTree .com.

Introduction

While I was sitting in the back of my Weight Watchers meeting, my phone notifications started piling up. Something I said while conducting teacher training a few days prior had gone viral. (By *viral*, I mean within one day of the original post, a meme attributed to my name had 6,200 reactions. There were well over 400 comments and 7,300 shares on one site.) Oh boy.

I'll be perfectly honest with you; my first thought was *I hope I didn't screw this up*. I scrambled to the internet, typed in some key phrases, and was unbelievably relieved to see that yes—numerous articles, education blogs, and reports backed up what I had said. Thank goodness.

You see, during that teacher training, I said, "Teachers make more minute-by-minute decisions than brain surgeons, and that is why you're going home so exhausted each day." Now, we can certainly argue the merits of my wording. For instance, I believe brain surgeons are called *neurosurgeons*, and I'm not sure we want said neurosurgeons making a whole lot of decisions when they're operating on our brains. However, my point is the average teacher makes 1,500 educational decisions every school day. In an average six-hour day in front of students, teachers make more than four educational decisions per minute (BusyTeacher.org, n.d.), and that is exhausting.

Next, I made a fatal decision—I started to read the comments. I know it was foolish. I really do know better than to do this. I once heard someone say reading the comments is like eating a sandwich that might have broken glass in it, but I did it anyway. For every wonderful shout-out to a teacher, there were (grammatically incorrect and wildly misspelled) posts about how lazy teachers are (only teaching half the year); how these data are stupid; how teachers are dumb; how my last name, Boogren, looks like *booger*; how teachers are overpaid; and on and on—*and I couldn't stop reading them.* I felt exposed and vulnerable. (Let me remind you that I was at a Weight Watchers meeting, stripped down to my tank top and shorts to get on the scale in front of a stranger—as if I didn't already feel vulnerable enough.)

I was devastated. These comments simply were not in line with my worldview. They didn't match my experience as a lifelong educator and an educational researcher, nor did they match the data regarding teacher retention. Those data claim that the profession loses 50 percent of new teachers within the first five years due to excruciating demands; 4 percent *more* professionals than other professions; and 15.7 percent of teachers every year, with fewer than 34 percent leaving for retirement (Riggs, 2013; Westervelt, 2016).

Finally, I thought, *I have something to say here. I deserve to respond to these comments for the sake of all the amazing educators I have the honor and privilege of working with, but I refuse to get into an online shouting match.*

So my response to the naysayers is that I've worked with a lot of teachers in my career. Do I fully admit there are some very bad ones in the mix? You bet I do. I've seen them. I've coached them. They've made me cry. Can I tell you story after story about the ridiculous things they do? I could go on and on—but I choose not to, because for every teacher who isn't enhancing the profession, ten others are working their tails off to be intentionally inviting to their students, often to the detriment of their own families, health, and sanity (Boogren, 2012; Novak & Purkey, 2001). These teachers need someone to acknowledge the incredible demands and pressures felt in schools and classrooms all over the country because the public often has a skewed view of the job's realities. And when the public thinks they understand a teacher's job, they feel like they have the right to comment, judge, evaluate, and criticize, and that is crushing to the hardworking educators I've had the pleasure of working with.

The reality is that teachers are public servants, and people have a right to share their opinions about teachers just as they do about police officers, doctors, and government officials. But criticism hurts when you intimately know the other side. For teachers, that side includes the hours revising lesson plans to ensure challenging advanced students while simultaneously scaffolding students who need more time. It's the late nights at school coaching, grading, planning, sponsoring, cheering, meeting, and fretting. It's having trouble feeling fully present with your family because students also feel like family and, when you're not with them, you're not sure how much love they're getting. It's having trouble feeling fully present with students because you're carrying guilt about spending the evening at home grading papers, creating lesson plans, and responding to emails and texts from students and parents. It's paperwork, paperwork, paperwork. It's figuring out how to provide feedback that strikes the precarious balance between loving and pushing—between pointing out what's correct and being honest about what's off the mark. It's the hours spent with colleagues focused on one student, when ten more need that same attention. It's presenting a lesson while also being aware of each student's behavior in your classroom so you can direct the appropriate attention, support, love, and discipline each student needs. It's testing and assessing, and knowing that both the students and their teachers will face unfair consequences because of one test. It's having a perfect day when no one visits your classroom, and having everything fall apart when twelve visitors arrive for instructional rounds. It's setting up field trips, guest speakers, and parent volunteers—tasks so monumental that planning a wedding feels like a piece of cake in comparison. And that's only some of it.

I continually contemplate the question, "How else can I help ease the burden, lighten the load, honor the work, and sing the praises of hardworking, dedicated, and passionate educators beyond what I provide during my professional development training?"

I now have the answer.

What Self-Care Is

I believe, in my heart of hearts, that the key to thriving—as both a human being and an educator—rests in self-care. To be clear, that is *daily* self-care, not the kind we promise to do during the summer or on the weekends, or when our own children are older, or when we retire. Yes, *daily*. Psychologist Catherine

P. Cook-Cottone (2015) defines *self-care* as the "daily process of being aware of and attending to one's basic physiological and emotional needs including the shaping of one's daily routine, relationships, and environment" (p. 297). These include small tweaks, reminders, and (perhaps most important) *permission* for educators to take care of themselves.

Educators read lots of books and engage in lots of professional development for the sake of student achievement, and they should continue doing so. However, I propose a radical shift in thinking. What if teachers learn to take care of themselves *while* taking care of their students? What if it weren't an either-or situation? What if you split your time between your own and students' needs in a new way? What if, for every move you make for the sake of your students, you also make a move for your own sake? What if you not only engaged in professional development on pedagogy and content, but also spent time learning how to best support yourself?

On average, I travel by airplane at least twice a week to work with educators all over the United States and I hear this line during the safety demonstration on every single flight, no matter the airline: "Secure your own oxygen mask before assisting others." This is the essence of what I'm talking about. All human beings—particularly parents, public servants, and caregivers—must take care of themselves before they can take care of others. In this incredibly demanding, often thankless, vocation, how can we expect educators to take care of students if they are not caring for themselves first? Here's what I know to be true above all else for educators: *research-based educational strategies and pedagogy are only as good as the person providing them.* And if the human providing the strategies is so depleted, worn out, and burned out that he or she can hardly breathe, then the expectation that he or she can provide oxygen to students is unrealistic. And yet this is what we are asking educators to do, day in and day out. So many are struggling to stay afloat, without the tools to learn how to properly thrive.

My goal is to help you create rituals, routines, procedures, habits, and mind shifts. This book presents *reminders* of ways to take care of yourself—about how getting enough sleep is an essential part of being an effective educator, as is pausing to take three deep breaths at various points throughout the day. It's about giving yourself permission to *be imperfect*. Educators know these things, but along your teaching (and life) journeys, you might have chosen students over yourself so many times that you've forgotten what it means to engage in consistent self-care without guilt. It's time to ditch the guilt.

You're overdue to take time for you.

What You Can Find in This Book

To begin, you'll gather some baseline data using two essential forms in chapter 1: a "Self-Care Survey: Starting Point" and a "Daily Time Audit: Starting Point." It's important to complete both so you know where you currently are. No matter what your initial results reveal, if you're willing to commit to this book's self-care practices, I promise you'll recognize a substantial improvement in well-being when you return to these same forms in the epilogue.

For the framework, I use Abraham H. Maslow's (1943, 1971) easily recognized and well-established theory of motivation. I present the framework as a ladder (instead of the more common pyramid), so you can visualize yourself climbing as you learn how to take exquisite care of yourself. As poet Jalaluddin Rumi (n.d.) suggests, "Be a lamp, or a lifeboat, or a ladder." Let this book be your ladder.

In each chapter, I'll help you become aware of when your needs aren't met and share specific strategies to help put you solidly on that particular level. After fully understanding the framework itself (chapter 1), you'll start at the ladder's first rung, where you'll get back to your body's basics—your physiological needs (chapter 2). You will write a personalized action plan for this first level and, after trying it for one week, reflect on how things went. From there you'll follow the same process and move up the ladder to safety needs (chapter 3), belonging needs (chapter 4), and esteem needs (chapter 5). After you stabilize the first four rungs, you'll move to the top two levels—self-actualization (chapter 6) and transcendence (chapter 7)—where personal growth occurs so you can move from merely surviving to truly thriving. Last, as stated in "Epilogue: Final Thoughts," you'll revisit the "Self-Care Survey" and "Daily Time Audit" so you can celebrate your growth and reflect on your progress.

Who Can Use This Book

This book is truly for *all* educators, not just teachers. That being said, it's important to note that this book also works for *everyone*, not just educators. Consider whether your noneducator family and friends could benefit from a dedicated focus on self-care. (I'm guessing they can.) While I provide examples that will appeal to educators, the framework and the action plans work for everyone.

You may choose to work with an accountability group or partner if that's helpful to you. The options are endless here. Perhaps your professional learning community, department, or grade-level team wants to do this work together; maybe you and a colleague decide to support each other; or perhaps you and your mentor or instructional coach want to work side by side. I've included guidance for groups and pairs in each chapter.

How You Can Use This Book

This isn't a traditional book that you will sit down and barrel through. Instead, this text is for savoring; it serves as both your guide and your anchor. It should start to look rugged from the time you spend reading and writing in it. You'll take it to school, then home, and then back to school.

Work through the chapters consecutively. You may end up spending more time with some chapters than others, depending on your starting results. For example, if your level one needs are fairly solid, you may spend less time there than you will on the following chapters. On the other hand, "a person who is lacking food, safety, love [belonging], and esteem"—consecutive crucial elements of the first four need levels—"would most probably hunger for food more strongly than for anything else" (Maslow, 2000, p. 254).

Don't skip chapters, as each level builds on the previous one. Commit to following your action plan for one week, and then return to the book for reflection and next steps. You might need an additional week with the same action plan, or you might want to stay at the same level but create a different plan, or you might be ready to move on to the next level. This is *your* guide, so you are free (and encouraged) to move at your own pace. There is space for you to write directly in the book so it is easy to dig into the work without the added distraction of a separate notebook. (Of course, you may use your own journal or digital space for action planning and reflections if that is your preference.)

It is essential that you do the work. Simply reading about the levels and strategies will *not* improve your life. Set a clear intention and commit to this journey. It may take you a few weeks or a few months to complete the book. Either way, doing the work is the most important part. This work is messy. There will be weeks you won't engage as much as you'd like, and that's OK. Don't let a desire to be perfect stop you from picking yourself back up and jumping back in at any point.

Your Pre-Engagement

Congratulations—your journey to your improved life begins today! Thank you for joining me in this work and for giving yourself this gift. Rather than trying to engage with this content perfectly, plan for possible failure so you can *avoid* it. To help do that, respond to the following questions.

Why do you have this book in your hands right now? What is your greatest hope for doing this work?

....

....

What will prevent you from engaging in this work? (Examples include getting sick, your children getting sick, feeling too overwhelmed to spend time on it, and comparing yourself to others and feeling you're not doing it right.)

....

....

Now that you've identified why you might struggle, how can you overcome these obstacles? Why will this time be different? What is your plan for sidestepping your usual challenges and frustrations?

....

....

Congratulations! By responding to these initial questions, you just identified possible snags that kept you from doing work like this in the past. This time, however, will be different. Now you are prepared to tackle these obstacles head-on, knowing that life—especially as an educator—is never perfect and our time can easily be consumed by other projects, lists, and people. As you begin this journey, keep your responses to these questions close by (maybe put a sticky note on the pages) so you can return to them when life feels like it's getting in the way of this work.

CHAPTER 1
The Foundation

And so it begins. Today is when you begin moving from surviving to thriving, both inside and outside of your school or classroom. Congratulate yourself for choosing you. You deserve this. You are worthy. Remind yourself of this when you feel like going back to your old life. We are going to take this incredible journey together and all the hard work you put into yourself will be worth it. Now take a deep breath; let's get started.

Before you work on improving your own life, you'll need to get an unbiased sense of where you currently are, which we'll do in this chapter. From there, we'll dig more deeply into humanist psychologist Abraham H. Maslow's (1943) hierarchy of needs and how this framework applies to humanity as a whole, as well as to you, an educator.

Foundation Strategies

Buddha says that, "if you want to know your past life, look at your present condition. If you want to know your future life, look at your present actions" (Good Reads, n.d.). So here we are, taking a look—an honest look—at your present actions. Don't skip this part. Instead, honor it. Give yourself the grace of alone time to give your undivided attention to the following tasks, without judgment. Know that whatever you discover from the following exercises is fine. You are enough, exactly as you are, in this current moment. Even if you're working with an accountability partner or group, gathering your own starting data is solo, private work.

When I started my own self-care journey, I reflected on my current situation, just as I'm asking you to do. This proved vital in understanding and identifying exact places where I needed to make some changes. For example, I've always been a pretty good sleeper and thought I did a fairly good job of getting my seven hours of sleep each night. Only when I started monitoring my sleep habits (with my Fitbit device) did I discover that most nights I was getting six or fewer hours. When I learned this, I made sleep a physiological priority in my action plan. I also discovered that I wasn't speaking very kindly to myself (an esteem need). In fact, that inner voice was more vicious than kind, and I learned that I needed to change that self-talk if I wanted to stabilize my own ladder.

Carve out some quiet time for yourself before continuing.

Your Starting Place

In this section, using two forms, you'll identify—and celebrate—areas where you're currently thriving and areas where you can grow. Complete both forms before moving to the other chapters.

Try not to judge your responses, as they are simply a means to see where you're starting so you can celebrate your growth as you move along your self-care journey. Remember that you are enough, no matter the results. You'll revisit these tools in "Final Thoughts" (page 117).

Self-Care Survey: Starting Point

For each statement in figure 1.1, check the box that reflects the frequency of your behavior within the past seven days. Don't get too hung up on the exact frequency, knowing that each week can be a bit different from the last. Instead, think about a typical week and give your best estimate as to how many times you engaged in the identified behavior within that seven-day period.

You'll notice that some statements mention *at home or school.* In those cases, think about both your work and your home environments. If you feel strong in one area (home, for example) but weaker in another (school, for example), you probably won't want to check a box that's higher than *Sometimes.* That helps give an accurate overall picture of *both* your work and your home life, because you know that one impacts the other in sometimes profound ways. For example, if you always feel safe at home but most days you feel unsafe at school due to an intimidating student or colleague, you will check a box on the lower (left) side of the scale. If, on the other hand, you feel extremely safe at home and fairly safe at school, you will check a box on the upper (right) side of the scale. After completing the survey, you'll respond to some reflection questions that help you make sense of your findings—both the celebrations and the opportunities for growth.

In the past week, how many days did you do the following?	Never (zero days)	Rarely (one day)	Sometimes (two to three days)	Often (four to five days)	Always (six to seven days)
Physiology					
I drank at least six glasses of water.					
I got at least seven hours of sleep.					
I ate a variety of nutritious foods from a range of food groups.					
I engaged in physical activity.					
Safety					
I felt safe at school.					
I felt safe at home or away from school.					
I felt a sense of order or consistency at school.					
I felt a sense of order or consistency at home or away from school.					
Belonging					
I felt included and respected at school.					
I felt included and respected at home or away from school.					
I felt like a coworker truly cared about my well-being.					
I felt like a family member or friend truly cared about my well-being.					

FIGURE I.I: SELF-CARE SURVEY: STARTING POINT. continued ⇨

Esteem					
I spoke kindly to myself.					
I felt competent in my job.					
I felt important at home or school.					
Someone recognized the work I do at school or elsewhere.					
Self-Actualization					
I set personal goals at home or school.					
I believed I could accomplish what I set out to do.					
I had a positive outlook on the future at home or school.					
I had a moment of flow or a peak experience (where I felt totally, completely happy and at peace) at home or school.					
Transcendence					
I felt inspired at home or at school.					
I did something at home or at school for someone else without anyone asking me to.					
I felt empathy toward someone else or I forgave someone at home or at school.					
I felt a sense of gratitude or engaged in mindfulness.					

*Visit **go.SolutionTree.com/instruction** for a free reproducible version of this figure.*

How did it feel to take this survey?

....

....

Were you surprised by the results? In what way?

....

....

In what area or areas are you thriving the most? How does this make you feel?

....

....

In what area or areas are you the most challenged? How does this make you feel?

....

....

Would the results have been different during other times of your life (for better or for worse)?

....

....

What areas do you want to focus on the most? Why?

....

....

Add any other reflections that you have here.

....

....

Daily Time Audit: Starting Point

When you begin making changes in your life, it is possible to get stuck on the issue of limited time. Similar to the way you did for the self-care survey, you're going to take a closer look at how you're actually spending time throughout a typical workday and weekend day. This helps you identify activities and obligations that satisfy you, as well as identify opportunities to engage your action plans (which we'll begin creating very soon).

When I did my own daily time audit, I was horrified to discover the amount of time I spent cruising the internet. I was spending hours (yes, multiple hours) each day mindlessly scrolling through Facebook, Instagram, Twitter, and Pinterest. While I appreciate the need to zone out, I did not want to lose ten hours a week to social media. You may discover that, like me, you are a bit addicted to social media. Perhaps TV shows, Netflix movies, or Candy Crush games consume much of your day. And you may decide that is time well spent. If you would rather spend some of that time doing something else, that discovery is a warning to make a change.

During one entire day, record the start and end times of *every* activity that you partake in. I know this feels tedious, but it is essential information to gather for stabilizing your ladder. Include a brief description of what you're doing (getting ready for work, meditating, exercising, driving to work, teaching, attending a team meeting, sleeping, reading, scrolling through your Facebook news feed, or eating lunch, for example). Also note how you feel while you're engaged in each activity (happy, bored, energized, or irritated, for example), and what value you place on each activity (high, medium, low, or neutral). For example, eating dinner with your family might be of high value to you, while attending a staff meeting after school might be of medium or low value to you depending on the content and delivery of those meetings. Once you've recorded at least one typical workday and one typical weekend day, spend some time reflecting on the questions for the "Daily Time Audit: Starting Point" (figure 1.2).

How much time are you spending on low-value activities versus high-value activities? Do your values reflect the amount of time spent?

....

....

Start and End Times	Activity Description	How I Feel	Value (High, Medium, Low, Neutral)

Source: Adapted from Mind Tools Content Team, n.d.b.

FIGURE 1.2: DAILY TIME AUDIT: STARTING POINT.

*Visit **go.SolutionTree.com/instruction** for a free reproducible version of this figure.*

When are you most energized? When are you most sapped of energy?

....

....

What activities contribute to your positive emotions? What activities make you feel negative emotions?

....

....

How do your feelings relate to your values? (For example, when you're doing something that feels good, do you also place a high value on that activity? Perhaps you feel good when you're pinning beautiful quotes on Pinterest but don't highly value this activity.)

....

....

How does your weekday audit differ from your weekend day audit?

....

....

Add any other reflections that you have here.

....

....

The Framework: Maslow's Hierarchy of Needs

Now that you've done the hard work of reflecting on your current status, let's focus on the framework that serves as your self-care guide. You may be familiar with this model, which is grounded in research and decades of study (Maslow, 1943, 1954). These needs are usually presented as a pyramid, with the most basic needs on the bottom. Maslow chose this hierarchical shape for the concepts because each level is generally unavailable until someone fulfills the needs related to the levels below it. The first four levels—(1) physiological, (2) safety, (3) belonging, and (4) esteem—define needs an individual must meet in order to avoid negative physical or psychological sensations. The next two levels—(5) self-actualization and (6) transcendence—both articulate a desire for personal growth. Rather than a pyramid, however, let's embrace the visual of a ladder to emphasize how each level builds on the previous one and helps you reach new heights (see figure 1.3).

Maslow (1943, 1971) defines each need level's requirements. *Physiological needs* include the most basic—food, water, sleep, and shelter, for instance. *Safety needs* include physical safety and financial stability. *Belonging needs* include friendships, group acceptance, and intimacy. *Esteem needs* include feelings about oneself, respect of others, and respect by others. *Self-actualization* includes realizing your full potential and personal growth in general, while *transcendence* includes connecting with something outside of yourself or, as Maslow (1971) puts it, "behaving and relating, as ends rather than means, to oneself, to significant others, to human beings in general, to other species, to nature, and to the cosmos" (p. 269).

Source: Adapted from Maslow, 1943, 1971.

FIGURE 1.3: MASLOW'S HIERARCHY OF NEEDS.
Visit **go.SolutionTree.com/instruction** for a free reproducible version of this figure.

To understand the framework even further, know that levels one and two are associated with attention. In other words, if your first two need levels are unmet, your thoughts focus on your basic physiological needs rather than what is occurring around you. Think about that slang term *hangry* (Francis, 2005). If you are so hungry that your blood glucose drops below healthy levels, you become angry—*hangry*—and more likely to lash out (Bushman, DeWall, Pond, & Hanus, 2014). That's the perfect example of what happens when your level one needs are unmet *quickly*—it is incredibly difficult to think about anything else besides finding food. Or imagine the fire alarm starts going off as you're reading this sentence. Suddenly, your level two safety needs are threatened, and it is impossible for you to pay attention to this text. Think about the results of your self-care survey. If you had lower scores associated with the first two levels, you're probably having a difficult time just paying attention to your job or your life outside school. If your levels three and four needs are unmet, but levels one and two are solid, you might be able to attend to what is occurring around you, but you probably are significantly disengaged. For instance, if you are at a party where you don't know anyone but everyone else is part of the same friends group, you might not feel like you belong or like your expertise is valued. Again, consider the results of your self-care survey. If levels one and two were fairly solid but you scored lower for the second and third levels, determine if you're not fully engaged at school or at home as a result.

If your first four levels are solidly met, you can pull yourself up to the ladder's fifth and sixth rungs, where you can experience self-actualization and, eventually, transcendence. At these levels, you're not only attentive and engaged but also motivated and inspired. At levels five and six, you are truly thriving. If your self-care survey revealed high scores for every level, you are living a fulfilled life committed to helping others. That is something to be incredibly proud of.

It is important to note that at times you *can* engage in a higher level even though you have some unmet needs. This is really good news. For example, you can probably manage to have a good time while out with friends even though you might be really tired—thank goodness. If you have an occasional unmet need, the corresponding rung may weaken, but you can still stand on it to reach for the next-higher rung. However, if you have a consistently unmet need, the corresponding rung will eventually break completely. That makes the next level unreachable until you repair the rung.

Before getting into the strategies, spend some time answering the following questions. They will help you reflect on your current ability to turn inward and check in with yourself.

How do you currently check in with yourself, and how often are you able to do this throughout your day?

....

....

How does understanding the needs levels help you understand yourself better?

....

....

Needs Identification Strategies

Metaphorically, you might say human beings in any given situation are constantly asking themselves the questions in figure 1.4.

If you come upon a question you cannot affirm, you get stuck at that level. For example, if you ask yourself, "Are my basic needs met?" and respond with *Yes*, you'll move to the next question: "Do I feel safe?" If you respond with *No*, your brain will try to change that unsafe feeling rather than move on to the next question: "Do I feel like I belong?"

Do I feel connected to something greater than myself?

Am I living my best life?

Do I feel confident?

Do I feel like I belong?

Do I feel safe?

Are my basic needs met?

Source: Adapted from Maslow, 1943.

FIGURE 1.4: IDENTIFYING NEEDS.

*Visit **go.SolutionTree.com/instruction** for a free reproducible version of this figure.*

The framework (figure 1.3, page 17) and these questions (figure 1.4), which you'll refer to throughout this book—and, ideally, in the future—become your guide to self-care. You may have to learn to check in with yourself on a regular basis to recognize when you're feeling off—angry, irritated, frustrated, uncomfortable, or anxious, for example. From there, run through these questions, starting at the bottom, and move your way up. When you know exactly where you're stuck, you can respond with targeted strategies.

Here's an example from my life. While in the grocery store, I felt tense and frustrated because the woman in aisle three wouldn't move her cart to the side, the man in aisle six was hollering on his phone, and the shelves in aisle seven didn't have the LaCroix sparkling water I craved. As an overblown result of these minor annoyances, I basically hated everyone and everything. I huffed and puffed audibly, threw my arms around in a dramatic and ridiculous way, and felt my heart rate steadily rising.

But I caught myself. I felt my negative emotions and paused just long enough to see myself from the outside. I recognized that I was unpleasant to be around right then. I ticked through the framework's questions and discovered that my negative feelings didn't stem from these minor grocery store setbacks. The true problem was my level one needs were unmet; I was struggling on four hours of sleep, no food, and too many cups of coffee. When all my needs are met and I can positively answer each framework question, those small grievances bounce off much more easily. But when something is off, I'm more likely to respond negatively.

How did I engage in self-care then, in aisle eight of my local Safeway? I took three deep belly breaths, chugged the water I had in my cart (paying for it at checkout, of course), and made a plan to eat before moving on to my next errand. It worked. My mood began to lift almost immediately.

What does all of this mean to you as an educator? Picture this: it's passing period and you have a chance to check in with yourself. When you do, you realize you do not feel awesome at all. In fact, you feel tense, annoyed, and ready to snap at the next person who asks you a question. Now that you know there's something amiss, you ask yourself the questions, starting with level one: "Are my basic needs met?" You answer *Yes*. You move to the next question: "Do I feel safe?" When you determine the answer is *Yes*, you ask, "Do I feel like I belong?" Here's where you stop, because you answer with a resounding *No*. Your teammates got together over the weekend but didn't invite you. You're actually hurt and sad and, as a result, in an incredibly foul mood.

You have a number of options that can help you answer this question more positively. You think about the people you care about most in life and text them to see if they're available to meet for coffee after school. Now you feel a slight shift. Rather than getting stuck on your feelings of not belonging to a certain group, you move your thoughts to people you truly belong with and plan to see one of them soon. You start your next class feeling better.

Or consider this scenario: you check in with yourself after pulling into the school parking lot but before getting out of the car. You realize that you feel amazing. You roll through the questions and get to answer *Yes* all the way up the ladder. Now you feel even more amazing because there's something beautiful about recognizing when things are going well *when they're actually going well.*

Knowing that you're the best version of yourself when the majority of your rungs are solid, pause to consider how exactly you will engage in self-care during your day. How and when will you check in with yourself and your body? Perhaps you want to start a habit of pausing when you pull into the school parking lot, before getting out of your car, and eventually you'll also commit to checking in with yourself during passing periods, at lunch, or every time the bell rings.

As you saw in figure 1.3 (page 17), an educator who is thriving feels good enough to help others—including students—move up their own ladders (level six). Thriving teachers are likelier to stay in the profession rather than become part of the 50 percent who leave within the first five years of teaching (Riggs, 2013). Beyond this claim, also consider the important implications for students. If a teacher has consistently unmet needs that force him or her to merely go through the motions, the classroom environment doesn't foster engagement, which affects student achievement and learning (Cardwell, 2011). High academic achievement is directly related to high classroom engagement (Gunuc, 2014), and teachers' engagement is directly related to students' (Cardwell, 2011). Plus, high student engagement increases a student's own sense of belonging at school (Gunuc, 2014). More than one person's needs are being met in a wave of engagement, which is what level six is ultimately all about.

And now, let's take time for you.

My Action Plan: Turn Inward

This chapter's prompts help you get in the habit of checking in with yourself to ensure your needs are met. Because our days are so busy, we sometimes forget to check in with ourselves. We're going to change that, starting now. You don't even need to do anything else at this point except learn to turn inward so you know when you're feeling good and when you're not. So many educators live in their heads for much of the day and have forgotten what it feels like to also live in their bodies. Print multiple copies of the framework (figure 1.3, page 17) or framework questions (figure 1.4, page 19) that resonate most with you, and place them around your home and classroom or office—maybe even in your car. Seeing them often will remind you to pause.

Pairing behaviors that you already have with behaviors you want to make habits—like checking in with yourself—will help you effectively make those actions habitual. As you know, our best intentions don't always result in lasting efforts. When you pair behaviors with established habits, the odds of the new actions becoming long term increase; research shows that it takes about sixty-six days to establish the new habit (Gardner, Lally, & Wardle, 2012). Researchers actually define habits as automatically triggered actions that we do when a particular contextual cue is associated— for example, "automatically washing hands (action) after using the toilet (contextual cue), or putting on a seatbelt (action) after getting into the car (contextual cue)" (Gardner et al., 2012). That means that eventually, if you ask the framework questions when you're doing something like checking your messages or going to the bathroom, you won't even have to consciously think about checking in with yourself.

For further help establishing this new habit, answer the following. Visit **go.SolutionTree.com/instruction** to download a free reproducible version of these prompts.

- I will notice how I feel at least _____ (*three, five, ten*) times per day.

- To remember to check in on how I feel, I will _____ _____ .

  - Set a reminder on my phone.
  - Download and use a phone app such as Chime (https://apple.co/2q91FHs).
  - Make a note in my calendar.
  - Stick a note to my mirror.
  - Pair events (such as going to the bathroom or eating) to my check-in.

- When I check in with myself, I will get in the habit of asking myself the following questions, in this order.

  - "Are my basic needs met?"
  - "Do I feel safe?"
  - "Do I feel like I belong?"
  - "Do I feel confident?"

- o "Am I living my best life?"
- o "Do I feel connected to something greater than myself?"

When I answer *Yes* to a particular framework question, I will record here how that makes me feel (*energized and calm, connected to those around me, as if I'm making a difference*).

....

....

When I answer *No* to a particular framework question, I will pay attention to how it makes me feel *and* how this unmet need manifests itself in me (*I get crabby, I make poor decisions, I am irritable, I feel restless and distracted, I'm bored, I feel angry*). I will record my thinking here.

....

....

When I forget to check in with myself, I will frame my thoughts about that positively (such as, "Tomorrow is another day" or "Progress, not perfection"). I will refer to the positive reframing I write here if I need a reminder.

....

....

When I can answer *Yes* to all (or nearly all) the framework questions, I am willing to express gratitude and celebrate ("I am grateful for this moment," "I feel amazing right now and recognize how wonderful life is," or "I want to remember this feeling so I can return to it"). My celebration may sound like the thoughts I record here.

....

....

At week's end, answer the reflection questions on page 24 or 26.

REFLECTION QUESTIONS

When you can affirm most of the needs (framework) questions, reflect on your behavior and mood. What circumstances help you get there? Is there a particular day of the week or time of day you feel best?

—— •●• ——

When you *cannot* affirm most of the needs questions, reflect on your behavior and mood. What circumstances seem to hinder moving up the ladder? Is there a particular day of the week or time of day when you feel most challenged?

—— •●• ——

Which needs questions do you seem to struggle with the most? Which questions elicit a more positive response? Does this feel typical, or do you think this might change given different times of the year or other conditions?

—— •●• ——

Reflect on different stages in your life and how your own level of happiness connects with the framework. When have you been the most fulfilled? How far up the ladder have you gotten? Where would you like to be?

— NOTES —

REFLECTION QUESTIONS
FOR ACCOUNTABILITY PARTNERS AND GROUPS

Before meeting with your accountability partner or group, reflect on the following questions alone. When you meet with your accountability partner or group, have each person share his or her completed action plan, notes, and responses to the individual and group reflection questions.

How did working with a partner or a group help you this week?

—— •●• ——

What could your partner or group have done to help you in areas you struggled?

—— •●• ——

What kind of support would you like from your partner or the group in the coming weeks, and how can you ensure that happens?

—— •●• ——

What did you do to help your partner or others in your group?

—— •●• ——

What can you do to help your partner or others in your group that you didn't do this week?

— NOTES —

CHAPTER 2
Physiological Needs

The first rung of the ladder includes basic physiological needs—water, food, exercise, rest, and shelter. If your basic needs are unmet, you won't get very far. You may not have eaten breakfast because you woke up late. Or, you may have eaten a hearty breakfast of steel-cut oats, a hard-boiled egg, and a handful of almonds, which allows you to start your day strong, but if you've skipped lunch in lieu of tutoring a student, by 3:00 p.m. *your hunger needs are unmet.* What happens then? You probably have trouble paying attention to tasks at hand because you are truly hungry in that moment. In foundational research known as the Minnesota Starvation Experiment, physiologist Ancel Keys and his colleagues (Keys, Brožek, Henschel, Mickelson, & Taylor, 1950) report participants who are hungry suffer a myriad of negative symptoms, including listlessness, depression, and apathy (Carter & Watts, 2016). A blood-sugar drop can occur when you need protein or eat a lot of sugar. Those physical symptoms can lead to sweating, shakiness, or trouble concentrating (Thompson & O'Brien, 2014), none of which is helpful, particularly as an educator.

Then there's sleep. Its importance is all over the media because we're not getting enough of it and it's negatively impacting us. Almost a third of adults aren't getting enough sleep (Schoenborn & Adams, 2010). Compare days where you wake up feeling refreshed and rested to days you had fewer than seven hours (perhaps much less, and perhaps multiple nights in a row). Can you spot the difference? I bet you can. Inadequate sleep, which can be the result of simply not going to bed early enough or a deeper issue like suffering from sleep apnea, leads to more car accidents, heart and other health problems, depression, forgetfulness, and weight gain (Peri, 2014). The pervasiveness and problems are so significant the

Centers for Disease Control and Prevention (2015) declare insufficient sleep a public health concern.

Assuming you have the resources to meet these essential needs, self-awareness is the key to ensuring a solid first rung. Look at your "Daily Time Audit: Starting Point" (figure 1.2, page 15) and consider how much time you're spending on your basic needs each day. Do you prioritize eating healthfully, sleeping, and exercising? If not, what can you change? After reviewing my own "Daily Time Audit" and implementing my own turn-inward action plan, I set a few phone notifications to remember to check in with myself. I began asking myself what I needed when the notifications went off—a drink of water? Some protein? To shut my eyes for a few minutes (if possible)? To get more sleep tonight? Additionally, I worked to set myself up for success by ensuring enough time to eat breakfast every morning and having healthy snacks and a water bottle with me at all times. Perhaps that approach would work for you, too. If you find that your level one needs aren't met, do something! Go drink a full glass of water, take a quick walk between classes, make a deal with yourself to not eat a cookie until you've had a vegetable, or stay home when you're sick, rather than going to work and suffering through the day.

Before getting into the strategies, spend some time answering the following questions. They will help you reflect on your current physiology and personal feeling of wellness.

Are you able to distinguish true hunger from a simple desire to eat (from boredom, for example)?

....

....

Do you like to get exercise by yourself, or do you prefer having a partner? What about team sports?

....

....

Do you feel a deep need or desire to nap during the day?

....

....

Physiological Strategies

The following lists include sample strategies to meet your physiological needs on a regular basis, including diet, exercise, and sleep. You can't do all of these starting today, but you can choose one or two that will be *most* helpful to you in the moments your basic needs are unmet. Refer to this list when you create your action plan in the next section.

Diet Strategies

The following are diet-related sample strategies.

- Drink more water (Mayo Clinic Staff, n.d.).

- Eat a piece of fruit or snack on a vegetable (rather than grabbing a sugary or salty treat).

- Plan your meals ahead of time.

- Include protein in your next meal or snack.

- Pack your lunch to ensure a balanced midday meal.

- Pack your own snacks for meetings.

- Try a meal delivery service like Blue Apron (https://blueapron.com), HelloFresh (https://hellofresh.com), or Plated (https://plated.com).

- Shop the grocery store's outer aisles to avoid processed food (Bonci, 2009).

- Consider having your groceries delivered to ensure you have foods at all times that make you feel good. Many national chains offer delivery (Kroger and Ralphs, for example), as do some mom-and-pop stores.

- Carry your own water bottle at all times.

- Eat without distractions (LeWine, 2013).

- Cook your favorite dish or meal and double the recipe so you have leftovers for the following day.

- Replace soda with regular or seltzer water (Vartanian, Schwartz, & Brownell, 2007).

- Split a meal with a friend at a restaurant to help control portion size.

- Team up with a colleague and share healthy lunches. (One person brings enough for two on Mondays and Wednesdays, and the other person does the same on Tuesdays and Thursdays.)
- Use an app like MyFitnessPal (www.myfitnesspal.com) to record what you're eating and monitor your nutrition.

Exercise Strategies

The following are exercise-related sample strategies.

- Schedule exercise time in your calendar as you would a doctor's appointment.
- Sign up for a local charity run or walk.
- Engage in activities you loved as a child—ride a bike, hula hoop, or climb a tree.
- Suggest walking meetings.
- Keep tennis shoes at school so you can take a quick walk at any given moment.
- Walk the school track or inside the building wearing a pedometer, so you can monitor your steps per day (Tudor-Locke & Bassett, 2004).
- Engage in challenges with colleagues (such as the 30-Day Walking Challenge at http://undrarmr.co/2zFiQa7; search for "thirty-day challenges" online for others).
- Try a ClassPass (https://classpass.com) if it's available in your city. Try a variety of exercise classes to see what you like best; some gyms offer a free class trial or guest passes.
- Work outside.
- Try gardening.
- Take movement-based brain breaks alongside your students.
- Experiment with aerobic activities (like jogging) as well as anaerobic activities (like weight lifting or yoga) to see what you like best.

- Motivate yourself with a fitness tracker such as Fitbit (https://fitbit.com/home) or the Daily Challenge app (https://challenge.meyouhealth.com/signup).

- Park in the farthest parking spot.

- Take the stairs whenever possible.

Sleep Strategies

The following are sleep-related sample strategies.

- Set a reminder to go to bed earlier.

- Remove all electronics from your bedroom (Harvard Health Publishing, 2015).

- Take a short nap (fifteen minutes or fewer) during the day, if possible (Lovato & Lack, 2010).

- Make sure your neck is in a neutral position while sleeping.

- Go to sleep and awaken at the same time each day (even on weekends).

- Avoid caffeine six hours before bedtime (Drake, Roehrs, Shambroom, & Roth, 2013).

- Finish vigorous exercise three to four hours before bedtime (Myllymäki et al., 2011).

- Don't ingest heavy foods or big meals late in the evening (de Zwaan, Burgard, Schenck, & Mitchell, 2003).

- Start dimming your lights two to three hours before bedtime (Gooley et al., 2011).

- Try reading something calming, meditating, taking a warm bath, or listening to quiet music before bedtime.

General Physiology Strategies

The following are some other sample strategies you may find helpful.

- Keep extra clothing with you in case you need to cool down or warm up.

- Wash your hands regularly to help prevent illness (Mathur, 2011).

- Carry and use hand sanitizer when you can't wash with soap (Pickering, Boehm, Mwanjali, & Davis, 2010).
- Stand outside in the sunshine (Nair & Maseeh, 2012).
- Pet an animal (Beetz, Uvnäs-Moberg, Julius, & Kotrschal, 2012).
- Ask for a hug, a handshake, or a pat on the back (Uvnäs-Moberg, 2003).
- Chew gum to avoid mindless snacking.

Record any other physiological strategies that you use or want to try.

- ....
- ....

I used the following strategies to help ensure that I can usually answer *Yes* to the needs (framework) questions.

- I always keep an apple, nuts, or a protein bar on hand in case I get hungry.
- I often set a notification midday for *bedtime* if I find I'm sluggish and I need additional sleep.
- I sign up online for yoga classes so I am extra accountable for attending; the times show up on my calendar, plus I'm committed to the yoga studio and the instructor.
- I set out my vitamins and supplements in the evening so it's easy to take them in the morning.

Now that I've shared some of my go-to strategies, it's time to think about your own level one action plan and which strategies you want to focus on this week.

My Level One Action Plan: Physiological Needs

You can create your own action plan for this level, similar to what I did for myself.

1. Go back and circle all the strategies in this chapter that appeal to you, including those you may have added on your own. At this point, don't worry about how many you're selecting; simply choose any that sound good to you and record them in the space following. You can list the strategies exactly as I described them earlier or you can tap into your creative side by including pictures or doodles or finding photos online that represent the strategies.

....

....

....

2. Now narrow down your selected strategies to a reasonable number. Only you can determine what feels reasonable to you. Consider how much work each strategy entails, what your daily schedule looks like right now, and whether you want to choose strategies that feel easy or you want to choose ones that stretch you. List your selected reasonable number of strategies in figure 2.1 (pages 36 and 37).

3. Decide which days you plan to employ each strategy, putting a check mark under those days in the Goal row. If you are working with an accountability partner or group, answer the questions at the end of the action plan as well.

4. Keep your action plan with you for the next seven days. Track which days you employ your chosen strategies and make any notes you'd like. For example, you might record how different you felt after using the strategy, or that the strategy doesn't seem to have an impact yet. Keep your notes simple, so tracking stays manageable.

At week's end, answer the reflection questions on page 38 or 40.

Week _____

Strategy	Sunday	Monday	Tuesday	Wednesday	Thursday	Friday	Saturday
Goal							
Actual							
Notes:							
Goal							
Actual							
Notes:							
Goal							
Actual							
Notes:							

Goal						
Actual						
Notes:						
Goal						
Actual						
Notes:						

If you're working with an accountability partner or group:

How can your partner or group help with your accountability? (For example, can you check in with one another daily via text, via email, or face-to-face?) List your ideas here.

How can you help support your accountability partner or group? List your ideas here.

Source: Adapted from Mind Tools Content Team, n.d.a.

FIGURE 2.1: MY PHYSIOLOGICAL ACTION PLAN.

Visit **go.SolutionTree.com/instruction** for a free reproducible version of this figure.

REFLECTION QUESTIONS

After following your action plan for one week and utilizing your selected strategies, respond to the following questions to determine if they positively impacted your life and whether you need to stay at this level for another week or if you're ready to move to the next level.

What worked well for you this week? Why?

—— •••• ——

Where did you struggle? Why?

—— •••• ——

Did you use the selected strategies on the intended days? If so, how did that impact you? If not, why not? (Was it an issue of time, perhaps? Did something unexpected happen to you this week?)

—— •••• ——

What differences do you notice in how you feel throughout the day after implementing your strategies?

—— •••• ——

As you think ahead to next week, would it be helpful to stay at this level and either (1) engage in the same strategies again or (2) select different strategies to work on? Or is it time to move to the next level? How do you know?

—— •••• ——

As an educator, how does focusing on your own physiological needs impact your work at school? As a person, how does focusing on your own physiological needs impact your life outside of school?

—— •••• ——

Record any other thoughts related to your physiological needs strategies.

— NOTES —

REFLECTION QUESTIONS
FOR ACCOUNTABILITY PARTNERS AND GROUPS

Before meeting with your accountability partner or group, reflect on the following questions alone. When you meet with your accountability partner or group, have each person share his or her completed action plan, notes, and responses to the individual and group reflection questions.

How did working with a partner or a group help you this week?

— •●• —

What could your partner or group have done to help you in areas you struggled?

— •●• —

What kind of support would you like from your partner or group in the coming weeks, and how can you ensure that happens?

— •●• —

What did you do to help your partner or others in your group?

— •●• —

What can you do to help your partner or others in your group that you didn't do this week?

— NOTES —

CHAPTER 3
Safety Needs

Now take a look at the second level: safety. You can think of *safety* as being free from "risk of injury, danger, or loss" ("Safety," n.d.). Safety involves order, predictability, and fairness, which reduce the possibility of physical or emotional harm. Feeling unsafe can contribute to anxiety, which, if experienced over time or continuously, can negatively affect your digestive, nervous, and immune systems (Holmes, 2014). A doctor can help you determine if you have an anxiety disorder if you feel like you're really struggling here.

After you've satisfied your physiological needs, you will naturally seek out situations where you feel secure. Ultimately, you want to have a sense of perceived safety as well as actual safety. In other words, you want to *be* safe and also *feel* safe. Allow me to explain. Although I am not afraid to fly, I feel like I'm pushing my luck to climb onboard a large metal bird and ask it to get me safely to my destination. I think a lot of people feel this way, and those feelings can result in a lot of bad passenger behavior. Perhaps the guy yelling at the gate agent about the ten-minute delay is subconsciously stuck on the question, "Does this situation make me feel safe?" (Or maybe he isn't, but I do appreciate looking at the world this way because it helps make sense of people's so-called *bad behavior* and interpret a difficult situation in a new way.) And while the safety demonstration is there to make us safer, it reminds us what we're doing is not 100 percent safe (and thus has an impact on our perceived safety).

Safety can be connected to your sense of control. If you don't feel like you have control in a certain situation, you may feel unsafe as a result (Newsome, 2015, as cited in Maclay, 2016). For example, I know my husband has a difficult time being a car passenger because he would rather drive himself; otherwise, he doesn't feel safe. Of course, he doesn't usually articulate his feelings this calmly. Instead, he keeps a vice grip on the door handle, grits his teeth for the entire ride, and mutters under his breath. But I know him well enough to know what's actually going on, and we now have fewer arguments when I'm in the driver's seat.

School safety is top of mind, and reported violent events affect perceived safety. Actual risk for schools is low, however, since they are safer than ever. According to 2013 U.S. Department of Justice and U.S. Department of Education findings, safety improved and violence declined for both students and teachers by nearly every measure (Toppo, 2013). According to a School Improvement Network survey conducted shortly after the December 2012 Sandy Hook Elementary School shooting, 92 percent of teachers reported feeling safe at school. With gun violence at the forefront of many educators' minds, the goal is to create welcoming, safe spaces of learning for both the students and the adults.

It is a blessing when our safety needs are regularly met. When you have a secure job and a steady paycheck, insurance, a savings account, and protection from the elements, it is easy to answer *Yes* to the question, "Do I feel safe?" However, if you fear losing your job, struggle to make ends meet, lack health insurance, or lose your home, you are acutely aware of safety's importance and how difficult it is to pay attention when this level isn't secure.

Before getting into the strategies, spend some time answering the following questions. They will help you reflect on your current feelings of perceived and actual safety.

Do you tune into and honor your intuition when it comes to your safety?

....

....

Do you take unnecessary risks (including putting yourself in physically unsafe situations and putting off planning financially for the future)?

....

....

Is there a gap between your perceived and actual safety?

....

....

Safety Strategies

The following list includes sample strategies to meet your safety needs on a regular basis. You can't do all of these starting today, but you can choose one or two that will be *most* helpful to you in the moments you *do not* feel safe. Refer to this list when you create your action plan in the next section.

- Record your worries in a journal or book (Ullrich & Lutgendorf, 2002).

- Reach out and talk to someone about your worries or stresses (American Psychological Association, n.d.).

- Stick to a schedule if consistency feels calming to you.

- Listen to calming music, such as a station you preset on free apps like Pandora (www.pandora.com) or Spotify (https://spotify.com; Thoma et al., 2013).

- Inhale a calming essential oil such as lavender or geranium (Haze, Sakai, & Gozu, 2002; Toda & Morimoto, 2008).

- Try calming activities such as meditation, yoga, Tai Chi, and Pilates (Hoge et al., 2013; Smith, Hancock, Blake-Mortimer, & Eckert, 2007).

- Talk to a banker or financial adviser to ensure you're saving and investing wisely.

- Make sure you have a thorough understanding of your insurance policies—deductibles, copays, what's covered, and what isn't.

- Ensure your family has a safety plan; use the U.S. government's protocol (https://ready.gov/make-a-plan).

- Memorize essential phone numbers (rather than relying on your phone contacts).

- Make copies of your driver's license, passport, birth certificate, and so on, and store them in a safe place.

- Ensure you understand the emergency procedures in your school or workplace.

- Reflect on your daily activities and recognize where there is a lack of order. What can you do to bring consistency to that area of your life?

- Pay attention to your surroundings so you remain aware and know where the nearest exits are.

- Implement rules and procedures with a focus on safety (for students, yourself, and property) in your classroom or school.

Record any other safety strategies that you use or want to try.

- ....

- ....

Personally, I addressed this level's needs by using the following strategies.

- I meet with a financial adviser face-to-face at least once a year.

- I carry small vials of essential oils in my purse and inhale their calming scents before giving any presentations.

- I schedule regular medical appointments, including dental, dermatological, optometric, and so on.

- I regularly back up my computer and phone files to external sources as well as to the cloud.

- I meditate every morning and attend a Bikram yoga class at least once a week.

- I revamped my morning routine to allow extra time, implementing order and consistency into an important part of my day.

Now that I've shared some of my go-to strategies, it's time to think about your own level two action plan and which strategies you want to focus on this week.

My Level Two Action Plan: Safety Needs

You can create your own action plan for this level, similar to what I did for myself.

1. Go back and circle all the strategies in this chapter that appeal to you, including those you may have added on your own. At this point, don't worry about how many you're selecting; simply choose any that sound good to you and record them in the space following. You can list the strategies exactly as I described them earlier or you can tap into your creative side by including pictures or doodles or finding photos online that represent the strategies.

    ....

    ....

    ....

2. Now narrow down your selected strategies to a reasonable number. Only you can determine what feels reasonable to you. Consider how much work each strategy entails, what your daily schedule looks like right now, and whether you want to choose strategies that feel easy or you want to choose ones that stretch you. List your selected reasonable number of strategies in figure 3.1 (pages 48 and 49).

3. Decide which days you plan to employ each strategy, putting a check mark under those days in the Goal row. If you are working with an accountability partner or group, answer the questions at the end of the action plan as well.

4. Keep your action plan with you for the next seven days. Track which days you employ your chosen strategies and make any notes you'd like. For example, you might record how different you felt after using the strategy, or that the strategy doesn't seem to have an impact yet. Keep your notes simple, so tracking stays manageable.

At week's end, answer the reflection questions on page 50 or 52.

Week _____

Strategy	Sunday	Monday	Tuesday	Wednesday	Thursday	Friday	Saturday
Goal							
Actual							
Notes:							
Goal							
Actual							
Notes:							
Goal							
Actual							
Notes:							

Goal						
Actual						
Notes:						
Goal						
Actual						
Notes:						

If you're working with an accountability partner or group:

How can your partner or group help with your accountability? (For example, can you check in with one another daily via text, via email, or face-to-face?) List your ideas here.

How can you help support your accountability partner or group? List your ideas here.

Source: Adapted from Mind Tools Content Team, n.d.a.

FIGURE 3.1: MY SAFETY ACTION PLAN.

*Visit **go.SolutionTree.com/instruction** for a free reproducible version of this figure.*

REFLECTION QUESTIONS

After following your action plan for one week and utilizing your selected strategies, respond to the following questions to determine if they positively impacted your life and whether you need to stay at this level for another week or if you're ready to move to the next level.

What worked well for you this week? Why?

— •●• —

Where did you struggle? Why?

— •●• —

Did you use the selected strategies on the intended days? If so, how did that impact you? If not, why not? (Was it an issue of time, perhaps? Did something unexpected happen to you this week?)

— •●• —

What differences do you notice in how you feel throughout the day after implementing your strategies?

— •●• —

As you think ahead to next week, would it be helpful to stay at this level and either (1) engage in the same strategies again or (2) select different strategies to work on? Or is it time to move to the next level? How do you know?

— •●• —

As an educator, how does focusing on your own safety needs impact your work at school? As a person, how does focusing on your own safety needs impact your life outside of school?

— •●• —

Record any other thoughts related to your safety needs strategies.

— Notes —

REFLECTION QUESTIONS
FOR ACCOUNTABILITY PARTNERS AND GROUPS

Before meeting with your accountability partner or group, reflect on the following questions alone. When you meet with your accountability partner or group, have each person share his or her completed action plan, notes, and responses to the individual and group reflection questions.

How did working with a partner or a group help you this week?

— •●• —

What could your partner or group have done to help you in areas you struggled?

— •●• —

What kind of support would you like from your partner or group in the coming weeks, and how can you ensure that happens?

— •●• —

What did you do to help your partner or others in your group?

— •●• —

What can you do to help your partner or others in your group that you didn't do this week?

— Notes —

CHAPTER 4

Belonging Needs

Oh, belonging. It's what everyone craves somehow, isn't it (Baumeister & Leary, 1995; Richman & Leary, 2009)? Everyone wants to be accepted, be part of a group, and have quality relationships. This is so incredibly easy to see in students. As a middle school teacher and administrator, I saw this daily. Especially at their fragile ages, students are desperate to belong (Brown & Larson, 2009)—so desperate, in fact, that if they *don't* feel like they belong, the consequences can be devastating, ranging from depression to self-injury and even suicide (Bearman & Moody, 2004).

These results aren't only true of middle school students, of course, as feelings of belonging—or a lack thereof—have a huge impact on your emotional health, no matter how old you are (Cacioppo & Hawkley, 2009). In fact, following seventy-five years of longitudinal research known as the Harvard Grant Study, psychiatrist George E. Vaillant (2012, as cited in Gregoire, 2013) finds "joy is connection . . . the more areas in your life you can make connection, the better." This is from a person whose life's work centers on studying the concept of happiness and life satisfaction.

I often have the opportunity to work with beginning teachers and am struck by how their sense of belonging can make the difference between staying and leaving a school. If beginning teachers feel as though they're truly part of the school community, they're much more likely to stay. Conversely, if beginning teachers never really feel like they truly belong, they're much more apt to leave (Ingersoll, 2012).

To understand this level even more, Brené Brown (n.d.) says:

> *Belonging is not* fitting in. *In fact, fitting in is the greatest barrier to belonging. Fitting in, I've discovered during the past decade of research, is assessing situations and groups of people, then twisting yourself into a human pretzel in order to get them to let you hang out with them. Belonging* is something else entirely—it's showing up and letting yourself be seen and known as you really are—love of gourd painting, intense fear of public speaking and all.

Yes, yes, yes! Everyone has done it. I distinctly remember morphing into what my friends liked and disliked when I was younger, pretending I liked certain music or hiding my love of books and writing utensils. In fact, this need comes before a sense of self-worth. Think about that. First, you have to truly belong, and *then* you can work on your own self-worth, which is the next level in the hierarchy of needs (esteem). In other words, first you find your people, and then you can truly shine.

The key piece to this level, then, is relationships. They provide a sense of community. Maslow (1943) says this about *belonging*:

> *Now the person will feel keenly, as never before, the absence of friends, or a sweetheart, or a wife, or children. He will hunger for affectionate relations with people in general, namely, for a place in his group or family, and he will strive with great intensity to achieve this goal . . . he will feel sharply the pangs of loneliness, of ostracism, of rejection, of friendlessness, of rootlessness. (p. 381)*

For example, I received a text from my friend letting me know her mom passed away. My friend knew her death was coming, but it still hurt. My friend and her mom shared a true sense of belonging—a relationship built on honesty, support, and love—being truly seen by one another. Author Glennon Doyle Melton (2016) aptly describes grief as "love's souvenir" (p. 205). In other words, grief is proof of belonging—truly belonging. To experience love is to belong, and to experience grief is to have belonged. This is like looking at the back of the ladder and seeing belonging from the opposite side. Once you have a real sense of it, and that gift is suddenly taken from you, profound grief is what must be left.

Remember, you can't move to the next level until you re-establish a sense of belonging. That is why grief is both horrendous and beautiful. As I think about my friend, I feel a tiny bit of comfort knowing that to have this grief means that she had a solid sense of belonging.

As an educator and a human being, how do you keep this level steady? By working on strong relationships with your family, friends, and colleagues. Because teachers spend so much time devoted to their students, they tend to sacrifice time with those they love at home. *Make time* to tend to your relationships. Schedule coffee dates, dinner dates, and walks around the park with a loved one. When you are with loved ones, be fully present. Resist the urge to multitask when you're with your significant other. In other words, don't send work emails at your child's soccer game; don't grade papers during the only evening with your girlfriend; and don't create lesson plans while you're at a game with friends. By being fully present, you give yourself and those you love the gift of belonging.

Private relationships are crucial, but it's also important to form relationships with colleagues. It can increase your sense of belonging at work (and increase your esteem; see chapter 5, page 71), and people who work with friends perform better at work and actually have fewer accidents (Rath & Clifton, 2007). Additionally, research finds that seventy-year-olds are satisfied for reasons directly related to being content with their work (Vaillant, 2012). Taking time for you now in regard to belonging will pay off in the long run.

Having both professional and personal relationships with colleagues helps solidify this rung on the ladder, and you can increase your chances of belonging through simple conversations, fun activities, and the like. Even something as simple as catching up on one another's lives as you eat lunch together can help build a sense of belonging within the school community. That community nurtures teamwork, which results in better decision making, more complex problem solving, enhanced creativity, and skill building (Blanchard, 2007). Researchers Megan Tschannen-Moran and Wayne Hoy (1998) agree that "faculty trust is an important aspect of the openness and health of school climate. It is related to the authenticity of both the principal's and the teachers' behavior."

During professional meetings, ensure adequate time to build relationships with one another. Have people share one thing they're grateful for that day before starting a staff meeting. Have people share one thing they really wish people knew about them.

When I conduct trainings with educators, I spend a good chunk of time at the very beginning of the day setting up various groupings for our time together—solo reflection, elbow partners, crosstown buddies, and small groups—to ensure a good mixture of people getting to know and work with one another. Participants introduce themselves and answer some personal questions (but not too personal, which could be uncomfortable and inappropriate) as a way to get to know one another in unique ways—even if they've been colleagues for years. I often use the following questions. Visit **go.SolutionTree.com/instruction** to download the free reproducible.

- If you could live anywhere, where would you live?

- What is your favorite book?

- What motivates you to work hard?

- If you could only eat one meal for the rest of your life, what would it be?

- What would you sing at karaoke night?

- When you were a child, what did you want to be?

- What makes you laugh the most?

- What is your strangest pet peeve?

- Who is your hero?

- What superpower do you wish you had?

When grouping people, I remind folks this isn't fluff. In fact, having participants share positive information with one another is a purposeful decision because "when people experience positive emotions . . . their thinking tends to become more creative, inclusive, flexible, and integrative" (Southwick & Charney, 2012, p. 32). What I love about this time is watching participants begin to relax, laugh, put a hand on a colleague's arm, or generally go on with the day knowing they now belong to various groups and can attend to the training content, since this need is met. I always regret it when time constraints force me to skip this activity.

I also personally form relationships with participants as quickly as possible. Coming in to do a single day of training is tough, and I know that I won't gain buy-in or engagement if my group doesn't trust me. To facilitate that trust, I am ready by the time the first participant walks in. I can spend my remaining time prior to presenting shaking hands, asking questions, making eye contact, and welcoming them to the day. I know firsthand the impact this has, because every once in a while, something goes wrong with my technology and I'm scrambling to prepare for our start time. In those cases I'm unavailable to meet anyone before the microphone is clipped to my collar. What a difference. It takes considerably longer to form relationships and ensure that all people, including me, feel like they belong—which is much more difficult to do from the front of the room, with a microphone attached to me.

My very best training days are those when it's clear the group felt a sense of belonging (and their foundational needs at the previous levels were also met), so I could help them feel a sense of esteem as educators (the next level up the ladder). When I can get my participants to talk with their groups in meaningful ways, they express gratitude. And because so many teachers mention this when they evaluate my training, I believe this type of connection isn't happening during the regular school day—at least not as often as we need.

Before getting into the strategies, spend some time answering the following questions. They will help you reflect on your current relationships and your own personal feeling of belonging.

Who do you spend the most time with? (You might revisit your "Daily Time Audit: Starting Point" [figure 1.2, page 15] to help pinpoint this.)

....

....

Are the people you're spending the most time with lifting you up or weighing you down? Are you able to be your true self when you're with these people?

....

....

Who do you connect with at school? Do you know something about your colleagues' personal lives? Do your colleagues know something about your personal life?

....

....

Who can you turn to when you're struggling? Who do you celebrate with?

....

....

Belonging Strategies

The following list includes sample strategies to meet your belonging needs on a regular basis. You can't do all of these starting today, but you can choose one or two that will be *most* helpful to you in the moments you *do not* feel like you belong. Refer to this list when you create your action plan in the next section.

- When you are with your family or friends, make a commitment to truly be *with* them—no technological device distractions (Rosen, 2012; Steiner-Adair & Barker, 2013).

- Put dates with loved ones in your calendar so you don't blow them off. Rather than assuming you'll find time to catch up with your partner, actually pencil in when that's going to happen—and hopefully it happens more than once a week.

- If you utilize social media, use it to create a sense of belonging for yourself (Henry, 2012). Join groups of like-minded people; ensure your friends or connections are people who lift you up, not those who depress you or make you feel insecure or less than. Connect with educators in other cities or countries or follow those who inspire you on social media.

- When you have dinner with friends or family members, set up this challenge: everyone puts his or her phone face down in the center of the table. The first person who reaches for the phone has to buy dinner for the whole group.

- Start a positive email exchange with your group. Each day, each person sends an email with +++ in the subject line. In the body of the email, share three positive things about your day.

- Consider joining community groups having to do with a shared interest or passion. Consider recreation leagues, book clubs, Meetup (https://meetup.com) groups, religious organizations, arts organizations, or the like (Vincent, 2016). Be open to meeting new people.

- Let go of toxic relationships or relationships that no longer serve you. *Toxic relationships* are ordinarily defined as those where the other person does not wish you well or generally affects you negatively (Glass, 2015).

Record any other belonging strategies that you use or want to try.

- ....
- ....

I selected the following areas to help stabilize this particular level in my own life.

- I dropped one book club because I didn't feel connected with the members. I joined a different book club with women I truly connect with. I make it a priority to read the book and attend our dinner meetings each month.

- I put my phone away when I'm with my friends or family members.

- My husband and I have a commitment to go on at least one date night—just the two of us—every single week.

- I stay connected with colleagues by attending happy hours, birthday parties, and other celebrations.

- I block or hide negativity (from people, groups, or news feeds) on my social media accounts.

- I schedule brunch dates, happy hours, coffee meetings, and so on in my calendar so I don't miss them or consider them less important than my other tasks and responsibilities.

Now that I've shared some of my go-to strategies, it's time to think about your own level three action plan and which strategies you want to focus on this week.

My Level Three Action Plan: Belonging Needs

You can create your own action plan for this level, similar to what I did for myself.

1. Go back and circle all the strategies in this chapter that appeal to you, including those you may have added on your own. At this point, don't worry about how many you're selecting; simply choose any that sound good to you and record them in the space following. You can list the strategies exactly as I described them earlier or you can tap into your creative side by including pictures or doodles or finding photos online that represent the strategies.

   ....

   ....

   ....

2. Now narrow down your selected strategies to a reasonable number. Only you can determine what feels reasonable to you. Consider how much work each strategy entails, what your daily schedule looks like right now, and whether you want to choose strategies that feel easy or that stretch you. List your selected reasonable number of strategies in figure 4.1 (pages 64 and 65).

3. Decide which days you plan to employ each strategy, putting a check mark under those days in the Goal row. If you are working with an accountability partner or group, answer the questions at the end of the action plan as well.

4. Keep your action plan with you for the next seven days. Track which days you employ your chosen strategies and make any notes you'd like. For example, you might record how different you felt after using the strategy, or that the strategy doesn't seem to have an impact yet. Keep your notes simple, so tracking stays manageable.

At week's end, answer the reflection questions on page 66 or 68.

Week _____

Strategy		Sunday	Monday	Tuesday	Wednesday	Thursday	Friday	Saturday
	Goal							
	Actual							
	Notes:							
	Goal							
	Actual							
	Notes:							
	Goal							
	Actual							
	Notes:							

Goal							
Actual							
Notes:							
Goal							
Actual							
Notes:							

If you're working with an accountability partner or group:

How can your partner or group help with your accountability? (For example, can you check in with one another daily via text, via email, or face-to-face?) List your ideas here.

How can you help support your accountability partner or group? List your ideas here.

Source: Adapted from Mind Tools Content Team, n.d.a.

FIGURE 4.1: MY BELONGING ACTION PLAN.

Visit go.SolutionTree.com/instruction for a free reproducible version of this figure.

REFLECTION QUESTIONS

After following your action plan for one week and utilizing your selected strategies, respond to the following questions to determine if they positively impacted your life and whether you need to stay at this level for another week or if you're ready to move to the next level.

What worked well for you this week? Why?

—— •●• ——

Where did you struggle? Why?

—— •●• ——

Did you use the selected strategies on the intended days? If so, how did that impact you? If not, why not? (Was it an issue of time, perhaps? Did something unexpected happen to you this week?)

—— •●• ——

What differences do you notice in how you feel throughout the day after implementing your strategies?

—— •●• ——

As you think ahead to next week, would it be helpful to stay at this level and either (1) engage in the same strategies again or (2) select different strategies to work on? Or is it time to move to the next level? How do you know?

—— •●• ——

As an educator, how does focusing on your own belonging needs impact your work at school? As a person, how does focusing on your own belonging needs impact your life outside of school?

—— •●• ——

Record any other thoughts related to your belonging needs strategies.

— Notes —

REFLECTION QUESTIONS
FOR ACCOUNTABILITY PARTNERS AND GROUPS

Before meeting with your accountability partner or group, reflect on the following questions alone. When you meet with your accountability partner or group, have each person share his or her completed action plan, notes, and responses to the individual and group reflection questions.

How did working with a partner or a group help you this week?

— •●• —

What could your partner or group have done to help you in areas you struggled?

— •●• —

What kind of support would you like from your partner or group in the coming weeks, and how can you ensure that happens?

— •●• —

What did you do to help your partner or others in your group?

— •●• —

What can you do to help your partner or others in your group that you didn't do this week?

— Notes —

CHAPTER 5
Esteem Needs

Welcome to the ladder's fourth rung. Maslow (1943, 2013) explains that everyone has a "need or desire for a stable, firmly based, (usually) high evaluation of themselves, for self-respect, or self-esteem, and for the esteem of others" (p. 7). *Self-esteem* is defined as "positive (high self-esteem) or negative (low self-esteem) feelings that we have about ourselves" (Stangor, 2014). As Maslow (1943, 2013) indicates, this level's needs include both how we think of ourselves and how others think of us. Because it's difficult to control how others see us, I ask you to spend most of your energy on what you can control: how you think about yourself.

Briefly then, consider the esteem of others, which includes a basic desire to feel appreciated and recognized. The desire to be more appreciated is a consistent theme I hear from educators. Whether by their supervisors, parents, or the public at large, most educators I speak with feel underappreciated for the work they do. A lack of acknowledgment affects perceptions, and "for most individuals, praise or acknowledgment provides an increase in esteem" (Schwartz, 2010). As humans, we have a "desire for reputation or prestige . . . recognition, attention, importance or appreciation" (Maslow, 1943, p. 382). The tough part is that these things are out of our control. Additionally, if we rely too heavily on the need for recognition or appreciation, our sense of esteem becomes tied to external sources, and this can easily lead to stress, hostility, and conflict (Crocker, 2002).

You do have some authority over your self-esteem. Before reading how to increase your self-esteem, add a check mark in the boxes next to the statements in figure 5.1 (page 72) that are true for you. This will give you a clear sense of how you see yourself.

❐ I believe in myself and my abilities.	❐ I excessively blame or criticize myself.
❐ I feel comfortable in my own skin.	❐ I excessively blame or criticize others.
❐ I know what I want and can clearly express my desires and needs.	❐ I feel superior or inferior to others.
❐ I can laugh at myself.	❐ I compulsively underachieve or overachieve.
❐ I take responsibility for my actions.	❐ I do not take responsibility for my actions.
❐ I express appreciation for and regularly praise others.	❐ I frequently feel victimized or jealous of others.
❐ I can make decisions independent of others.	❐ I dominate others, or I do not stick up for myself.
❐ I show ambition and enthusiasm related to my interests and goals.	❐ I focus on other people's lives (for example, by engaging in excessive gossiping).
❐ I am simultaneously optimistic and realistic.	❐ I take excessive risks.
❐ I accept compliments gracefully.	❐ I fear change and risks.
❐ I try new things and am comfortable with change.	❐ I am overly negative, or I am so positive it is unrealistic.
❐ I communicate well with others.	❐ I am extremely reactionary, or I lack emotion.
❐ I act independently, without a need for others' approval.	❐ I constantly compare myself to others.
❐ I learn from my mistakes.	❐ I engage in black-or-white thinking.
❐ I respect differences between perspectives.	❐ I have an inability to compromise, or I need to always be right.
❐ I recognize my own value.	❐ I frequently brag or lie in conversations.
❐ I am humble.	❐ I am overly defensive and combative.

Source: Adapted from Harrill, n.d.

FIGURE 5.1: HOW YOU SEE YOURSELF.

Count the number of statements you checked on the *left* side of figure 5.1 and record your total here: _____ of 17.

Count the number of statements you checked on the *right* side of figure 5.1 and record your total here: _____ of 17.

People with high esteem tend to develop specific traits, just as people with low esteem tend to develop specific traits (Marzano, Scott, Boogren, & Newcomb, 2017). Consider this: the left side of figure 5.1 indicates high-esteem traits, while the right side indicates low-esteem traits. High-esteem traits are considered helpful positives, while low-esteem traits keep you from feeling good about yourself. At various times, everyone exhibits behaviors from both sides. At this level, you're working to increase your esteem, moving some of your low-esteem thinking over to the positive side.

Now that you have a clearer sense of your level of self-esteem, consider how you can more positively regard yourself (especially if your results are not what you'd like them to be). How do you accomplish this? I've been using—and it's been working—the strategy of thought revision. After all:

> By definition, esteem is a product of one's thinking. As such, being able to identify and edit pessimistic or negative thoughts as they arise may be one of the most powerful tools students [you] have to build their [your] esteem. (Marzano et al., 2017, p. 65)

Thought revision means recognizing a negative or low-esteem thought and instantly replacing it with a more positive or high-esteem thought (Beck, 1995; Marzano et al., 2017). It's really that simple—and that powerful. It requires only two steps: (1) *thought recognition*, which is realizing when you're thinking about yourself in a negative way, and (2) *thought substitution*, which is replacing that negative thinking with other, more helpful thinking. For example, if I find myself saying, "I'll never get this project done," I can quickly recognize that as a negative thought about myself. That is thought recognition. From there, I can change my thinking to "I've done projects like this before and I've always gotten them done; this time will be no different." That is thought substitution. You have to be aware of your own thinking—*metacognition*—and whether your thinking in that moment is positive or negative. The thoughts you have influence the kinds of evidence you seek—in your work and in interactions with others (Beck, 1993; Dweck, 2006; Morin, 2016).

To see what kind of thoughts you have about yourself, begin a new daily time audit (figure 5.2, page 74) for thought awareness, and pay special attention to the new column, Esteem. Record your thoughts during each activity throughout the day and whether each thought reflects high esteem, low esteem, or neutrality. Consider doing this for one weekday as well as one weekend day to see if there are differences.

Start and End Times	Activity Description	Esteem (High, Low, Neutral)

Source: Adapted from Mind Tools Content Team, n.d.b.

FIGURE 5.2: DAILY TIME AUDIT: THOUGHT AWARENESS.

Visit **go.SolutionTree.com/instruction** for a free reproducible version of this figure.

What activities produced high-esteem thinking? In other words, what makes you feel your best? What activities resulted in low-esteem thinking? Did anything surprise you?

....

....

Are your thoughts more positive or negative when you're at school? What about when you're not at school? Why? How does this make you feel?

....

....

What activities help you feel your best? Where do you truly shine? Can you engage in these activities more frequently?

....

....

What activities make you feel bad about yourself? Is there a way to change these activities or to engage in them less often?

....

....

After reflecting on your thought patterns, you can use thought substitution to modify low-esteem thoughts. To begin, you must know, understand, and believe this: *negative, low-esteem thinking is based solely on your own interpretation*. It is not a fact. Just because you think something does not mean it is true. For example, you might think your colleagues are uninterested in your contributions during the meeting because everyone looks bored, but you have no idea if this is true. Consider *all* the possibilities that could be true: everyone is exhausted after a long day of teaching, people's body language or faces don't match what they're thinking, your colleagues think you're brilliant, and so on. When you believe thoughts are subjective and malleable, you can increase your own self-esteem, which is really good news.

Before getting into the strategies, spend some time answering the following questions. They will help you reflect on your current self-esteem and esteem of others.

Did you check more statements on the high-esteem (left) side or the low-esteem (right) side? How does this make you feel? Were you surprised by your results?

....

....

Do you have different senses of self-esteem in various areas of your life? For example, do you feel more confident at work than you do socially or at home?

....

....

If someone else were to complete this activity on your behalf, do you think those results would be the same as yours? Why or why not?

....

....

Esteem Strategies

The following list includes sample strategies to meet your esteem needs on a regular basis. You can't do all of these starting today, but you can choose one or two that will be *most* helpful to you in the moments you *do not* feel confident. Refer to this list when you create your action plan in the next section.

- Conduct an expectations check. Expectations may set up negative thinking and low-esteem thoughts, particularly if the expectations are unrealistic (Nezlek, Vansteelandt, Van Mechelen, & Kuppens, 2008). Make sure you're setting realistic expectations for yourself. For example, consider your expectations around grading, feedback, and unit planning with students. Would you put these same expectations on a colleague?

- Consider how true your thoughts are and whether they are based on assumptions or exaggerations rather than reality. It's easy to lose sight of certain situations. For example, do you assume that everyone else gets better evaluations than you? Have a friend help you recognize when your thinking is extreme or out of touch with reality; it's sometimes hard to recognize this on our own. Stress lowers in teachers who set realistic, achievable goals for themselves (Divine, 2017; Friedman, 2000).

- Recite self-affirmations. Focus on the things in life that you value most—family, friends, and independence, for example. Mass communication professor Christopher N. Cascio et al. (2016) say this grounds you and is "rewarding and pleasurable, and . . . it works because it acts as a defense mechanism by reminding us of the things in life that we cherish, thereby broadening the foundation of our self-worth" (as cited in Jarrett, 2015). However, some research indicates that "repeating positive self-statements may benefit certain people, but backfire for the very people who 'need' them the most" (Wood, Perunovic, & Lee, 2009).

- Try emotional accounting. When a low-esteem thought enters your mind, reframe it. Rather than telling yourself,

"This unit was a flop," you can reframe it into, "I tried my hardest to prepare for this unit but it didn't go as well as I'd have liked." Again, ensuring a realistic perspective here is crucial. Don't fall prey to cognitive distortions such as black-or-white thinking such as, "If I can't do this perfectly, it doesn't count" (Burns, 2008).

- Experiment with thought cessation. When a low-esteem thought enters your mind, say aloud, "No!" (Burns, 2008). Then think realistically about your belief and realize the negative thought was subjective—not reality. To make your thought cessation even more psychologically effective, talk to yourself using your name (Moser et al., 2017). Try saying, "No! Tina, your perception of how the unit went isn't accurate."

- Identify your triggers. Certain events or triggers can lead to low-esteem thinking. Review your new "Daily Time Audit: Thought Awareness" (figure 5.2, page 74) to determine which activities (or people or places) trigger you, and then make changes. For example, if you notice that your colleague Steven makes you feel bad when you have lunch with him, spend less time with him.

Record any other esteem strategies that you use or want to try.

- ....

- ....

I selected the following strategies to help stabilize this particular level in my own life.

- Before a big presentation, I choose an affirmation for myself. I write the affirmation on a sticky note, put it in my pocket, and refer to it throughout the day. I've used affirmations such as the following.

    o I've got this.

    o I have the qualities to be successful today.

    o I know what I'm doing.

    o My potential to succeed is infinite.

- I use reframing *a lot.* When my brain is going crazy with negative thinking, I force myself to stop and immediately change my thoughts. For example, rather than thinking, *I'm never going to get everything done that needs to get done today*, I stop and create this thought instead: *It's all going to get done. It always does.*

- I remain aware of how people impact my sense of self-esteem. If I can't cut these people out of my life, I arm myself before being in the same room with them. I take just enough time to consider what I can do to keep my self-esteem intact, and make a plan that usually goes like this: if he or she says _____, I will respond with _____.

Now that I've shared some of my go-to strategies, it's time to think about your own level four action plan and which strategies you want to focus on this week.

My Level Four Action Plan: Esteem Needs

You can create your own action plan for this level, similar to what I did for myself.

1. Go back and circle all the strategies in this chapter that appeal to you, including those you may have added on your own. At this point, don't worry about how many you're selecting; simply choose any that sound good to you and record them in the space following. You can list the strategies exactly as I described them earlier or you can tap into your creative side by including pictures or doodles or finding photos online that represent the strategies.

....

....

....

2. Now narrow down your selected strategies to a reasonable number. Only you can determine what feels reasonable

to you. Consider how much work each strategy entails, what your daily schedule looks like right now, and whether you want to choose strategies that feel easy or you want to choose ones that stretch you. List your selected reasonable number of strategies in figure 5.3 (pages 80 and 81).

3. Decide which days you plan to employ each strategy, putting a check mark under those days in the Goal row. If you are working with an accountability partner or group, answer the questions at the end of the action plan as well.

4. Keep your action plan with you for the next seven days. Track which days you employ your chosen strategies and make any notes you'd like. For example, you might record how different you felt after using the strategy, or that the strategy doesn't seem to have an impact yet. Keep your notes simple, so tracking stays manageable.

At week's end, answer the reflection questions on page 82 or 84.

Week _____

Strategy	Sunday	Monday	Tuesday	Wednesday	Thursday	Friday	Saturday
Goal							
Actual							
Notes:							
Goal							
Actual							
Notes:							
Goal							
Actual							
Notes:							

Goal							
Actual							
Notes:							
Goal							
Actual							
Notes:							

If you're working with an accountability partner or group:

How can your partner or group help with your accountability? (For example, can you check in with one another daily via text, via email, or face-to-face?) List your ideas here.

How can you help support your accountability partner or group? List your ideas here.

Source: Adapted from Mind Tools Content Team, n.d.a.

FIGURE 5.3: My esteem action plan.

Visit **go.SolutionTree.com/instruction** for a free reproducible version of this figure.

Reflection Questions

After following your action plan for one week and utilizing your selected strategies, respond to the following questions to determine if they positively impacted your life and whether you need to stay at this level for another week or if you're ready to move to the next level.

What worked well for you this week? Why?

—— •●• ——

Where did you struggle? Why?

—— •●• ——

Did you use the selected strategies on the intended days? If so, how did that impact you? If not, why not? (Was it an issue of time, perhaps? Did something unexpected happen to you this week?)

—— •●• ——

What differences do you notice in how you feel throughout the day after implementing your strategies?

—— •●• ——

As you think ahead to next week, would it be helpful to stay at this level and either (1) engage in the same strategies again or (2) select different strategies to work on? Or is it time to move to the next level? How do you know?

—— •●• ——

As an educator, how does focusing on your own esteem needs impact your work at school? As a person, how does focusing on your own esteem needs impact your life outside of school?

—— •●• ——

Record any other thoughts related to your esteem needs strategies.

— Notes —

REFLECTION QUESTIONS
FOR ACCOUNTABILITY PARTNERS AND GROUPS

Before meeting with your accountability partner or group, reflect on the following questions alone. When you meet with your accountability partner or group, have each person share his or her completed action plan, notes, and responses to the individual and group reflection questions.

How did working with a partner or a group help you this week?

—— •●• ——

What could your partner or group have done to help you in areas you struggled?

—— •●• ——

What kind of support would you like from your partner or group in the coming weeks, and how can you ensure that happens?

—— •●• ——

What did you do to help your partner or others in your group?

—— •●• ——

What can you do to help your partner or others in your group that you didn't do this week?

— NOTES —

CHAPTER 6
Self-Actualization Needs

Welcome. Here you are, my friend. You've steadily climbed your way up the first four rungs of the ladder, and your reward is to ask yourself, "Am I living my best life?" To further understand the concept of self-actualization, consider the following claims Maslow (2000) makes in defining those who are self-actualized.

- Superior reality perception, allowing accurate judgment of others and accepting uncertainty and ambiguity

- More tolerance of self and of others

- Greater appreciation and complex emotional reactions

- Increased identification with others

- Increased creativity

- Higher frequency of peak experiences

One of the rewards of standing on this rung is the increased chance of having a *peak experience*—a moment in life where everything is perfect (Maslow, 2015a). This kind of experience has you so caught up in the moment that time seems to stop and everything falls into place. Peak experiences are your best moments, and their memory stays with you.

Using the following prompt, Maslow (2000, 2015) talked with about 80 individuals and studied the written responses of 190 college students. The prompt defines a *peak experience*:

> *I would like you to think of the most wonderful experience or experiences of your life; happiest moments, ecstatic moments, moments of rapture, perhaps from being in love, or from listening to music or suddenly "being hit" by a book or a painting, or from some great creative moment. First, list these. And then try to tell me how you feel in such acute moments, how you feel differently from the way you feel at other times, how you are at the moment a different person in some ways. (Maslow, 2015, p. 71)*

Consider your own peak experiences in light of this prompt. First, identify and then record the most wonderful experiences of your life.

....

....

Then, record how you felt in these precise moments. Be as specific as possible. Consider especially what felt different from how you feel at other, more mundane times of your life.

....

....

I have a distinct memory of a peak experience in my own life: my wedding day. I know that sounds cliché, but here's what I remember: I paused just long enough to look around the room and felt in awe of how completely happy and incredibly grateful I was to have all the people I loved in the same room. I can pinpoint exactly where I was standing and the room's details in that moment. It was total bliss. I remember thinking that I wanted the clock to stop. I knew the moment was going to slip out of my hands so quickly. I was fully present and alive; I felt such immense gratitude in that moment.

You might have a peak experience memory of experiencing your child's birth, winning the state championship, having a late-night conversation with a loved one, or volunteering at the local homeless shelter. There is no right or wrong way for these experiences to occur. These moments are you standing on the fifth rung—when you are self-actualized. Maslow (1969) says, "any person in any of the peak experiences takes on temporarily many of the characteristics which I found in self-actualizing individuals. That is, for the time they become self-actualizers" (p. 86). Think of it this way: during a peak experience, you possess many, if not all, of the traits outlined on page 87. In these moments, you probably clearly perceive reality, fully accept yourself and those around you, and feel immense gratitude and appreciation for the moment. You may even feel especially creative or inventive.

According to Maslow (1969), peak experiences can present themselves if you experience the following.

- Changed views of yourself in a healthy direction (esteem!)

- Changed views of other people (esteem again)

- Changed worldview

- Greater creativity, spontaneity, expressiveness, and idiosyncrasy

- A feeling that life in general is worthwhile, even if it's usually drab, pedestrian, painful, or ungratifying

How can you invite more of these experiences into your life, then? How can you ensure, as often as possible, that you are self-actualizing? I believe that if we find ourselves feeling that life is worthwhile, see ourselves and others in a positive light, and fully express ourselves, then we are living our best lives.

As with all things related to the hierarchy of needs, make the initial levels as stable as possible. When you've achieved that, you can focus on achieving flow (Sahoo & Sahu, 2009). Being in a state of flow is a similar feeling to having a peak experience, and when you are in flow, you are fulfilled and happy (O'Brien, 2014). In other words, you are living your best life. Psychologist Mihaly Csikszentmihalyi (1990, 2008) describes *flow* as moments when you're so deeply engaged in an activity that everything around you disappears and you lose track of time.

I can recognize flow in myself when I'm writing. Many days, I can churn out a few sentences or paragraphs, but then I'm easily distracted by my Facebook feed, what my dog is doing, or my emails. Every so often, however, flow allows me to write for hours (or at least a whole lot of minutes) without stopping. I miss meals (which is unusual for me); I hold off on using the restroom for as long as I can; and when I break, I'm surprised so much time has passed. It's glorious! Being in flow has a lot of the same sensations as a peak experience: being fully present, engaged, content, calm, and happy.

You've probably seen your class in flow. Those glorious, rare days have students so deeply engaged in a project that they're surprised when the bell rings. That's the best, isn't it? That flow is a kind of mini peak experience. Not all flow is monumental (good writing days don't compare to my wedding day, for instance), but flow can certainly occur during a peak experience.

When flow is occurring, you'll recognize the following characteristics (Csikszentmihalyi, 1990, as cited in Oppland, 2016).

- Concentration is completely on the task.
- Clear goals and rewards are in mind.
- Time is sped up or slowed down.
- The experience is a reward or an end in itself.
- Effortlessness and ease abound.
- Challenge and skills are balanced.
- Actions and awareness merge; dwelling on self-consciousness disappears.
- There is a feeling of control over the task.

Before getting into the strategies, spend some time answering the following questions. They will help you reflect on your current self-actualization, peak experiences, and flow.

When do you experience flow? Are you reading? Dancing? Playing a game? Teaching a particular unit? Planning a presentation?

....

....

Record your own moments of flow. Do these moments have similarities?

....

....

Are there common characteristics that help you arrive at these flow moments?

....

....

Self-Actualization Strategies

The following list includes sample strategies to meet your self-actualization needs on a regular basis. You can't do all of these starting today, but you can choose one or two that will be *most* helpful to you in the moments you *don't* feel as if you are living your best life. Refer to this list when you create your action plan in the next section.

If you think of flow as mini peak experiences, you understand how inviting more can help you feel like you're truly thriving. Consider the following strategies to help you achieve flow more often and consequently increase your happiness (Babauta, 2008):

- Choose work you love, whether it is for your education career or something you like to do outside of school (Babauta, 2008; Vaillant, 2012, as cited in Gregoire, 2013).

- Choose an important task—something that you love, is challenging but achievable, and takes time (Csikszentmihalyi & Csikszentmihalyi, 1988; Vaillant, 2012).

- Find your best time. Is it in the morning before everyone wakes up? During an uninterrupted lunch hour or your planning time in the afternoon? In the evening after everyone is asleep? Experiment.

- Remove distractions. That includes your phone, tablet, iPad, computer, TV, Kindle, and so on. If it requires charging, makes a noise, or lights up, put it away—far away.

- Train yourself to stay focused on a particular task for an extended period of time. If you get distracted, just bring yourself back to this particular moment.

- Keep practicing each of the sample strategies listed here. Each of these strategies takes time, but as with most things, you improve with practice and will be rewarded with flow.

Record any other self-actualization or flow strategies that you use or want to try.

- ....

- ....

When I set a goal to achieve more flow in my own life, I used the following strategies.

- Because I write best early in the morning and later in the evening, I schedule time for it during those parts of the day. I answer emails and engage in more mundane tasks during the afternoon.

- When sitting down to write, I put my phone on Do Not Disturb mode, clear my desk space, and ensure that I have my water bottle on hand. I also make sure I'm comfortable physically.

- I set a goal for myself each time I write. It can be to write ten pages or a chapter. I promise to meet my goal—and I usually do. When I'm done, I consciously acknowledge the gift of that time, and when I walk away (and back into the real world), I feel self-actualized.

Now that I've shared some of my go-to strategies, it's time to think about your own level five action plan and which strategies you want to focus on this week.

My Level Five Action Plan: Self-Actualization Needs

You can create your own action plan for this level, similar to what I did for myself.

1. Go back and circle all the strategies in this chapter that appeal to you, including those you may have added on your own. At this point, don't worry about how many you're selecting; simply choose any that sound good to you and record them in the space following. You can list the strategies exactly as I described them earlier or you can tap into your creative side by including pictures or doodles or finding photos online that represent the strategies.

....

....

....

2. Now narrow down your selected strategies to a reasonable number. Only you can determine what feels reasonable to you. Consider how much work each strategy entails, what your daily schedule looks like right now, and whether you want to choose strategies that feel easy or you want to choose ones that stretch you. List your selected reasonable number of strategies in figure 6.1 (pages 94 and 95).

3. Decide which days you plan to employ each strategy, putting a check mark under those days in the Goal row. If you are working with an accountability partner or group, answer the questions at the end of the action plan as well.

4. Keep your action plan with you for the next seven days. Track which days you employ your chosen strategies and make any notes you'd like. For example, you might record how different you felt after using the strategy, or that the strategy doesn't seem to have an impact yet. Keep your notes simple, so tracking stays manageable.

At week's end, answer the reflection questions on page 96 or 98.

Week _____

Strategy		Sunday	Monday	Tuesday	Wednesday	Thursday	Friday	Saturday
	Goal							
	Actual							
	Notes:							
	Goal							
	Actual							
	Notes:							
	Goal							
	Actual							
	Notes:							

Goal							
Actual							
Notes:							
Goal							
Actual							
Notes:							

If you're working with an accountability partner or group:

How can your partner or group help with your accountability? (For example, can you check in with one another daily via text, via email, or face-to-face?) List your ideas here.

How can you help support your accountability partner or group? List your ideas here.

Source: Adapted from Mind Tools Content Team, n.d.a.

FIGURE 6.1: MY SELF-ACTUALIZATION ACTION PLAN.

*Visit **go.SolutionTree.com/instruction** for a free reproducible version of this figure.*

REFLECTION QUESTIONS

After following your action plan for one week and utilizing your selected strategies, respond to the following questions to determine if they positively impacted your life and whether you need to stay at this level for another week or if you're ready to move to the next level.

What worked well for you this week? Why?

—— •●• ——

Where did you struggle? Why?

—— •●• ——

Did you use the selected strategies on the intended days? If so, how did that impact you? If not, why not? (Was it an issue of time, perhaps? Did something unexpected happen to you this week?)

—— •●• ——

What differences do you notice in how you feel throughout the day after implementing your strategies?

—— •●• ——

As you think ahead to next week, would it be helpful to stay at this level and either (1) engage in the same strategies again or (2) select different strategies to work on? Or is it time to move to the next level? How do you know?

—— •●• ——

As an educator, how does focusing on your own self-actualization needs impact your work at school? As a person, how does focusing on your own self-actualization needs impact your life outside of school?

—— •●• ——

Record any other thoughts related to your self-actualization needs strategies.

— Notes —

REFLECTION QUESTIONS
FOR ACCOUNTABILITY PARTNERS AND GROUPS

Before meeting with your accountability partner or group, reflect on the following questions alone. When you meet with your accountability partner or group, have each person share his or her completed action plan, notes, and responses to the individual and group reflection questions.

How did working with a partner or a group help you this week?

— •●• —

What could your partner or group have done to help you in areas you struggled?

— •●• —

What kind of support would you like from your partner or group in the coming weeks, and how can you ensure that happens?

— •●• —

What did you do to help your partner or others in your group?

— •●• —

What can you do to help your partner or others in your group that you didn't do this week?

— Notes —

CHAPTER 7

Transcendence Needs

Here you are. You may (or may not) have arrived, and either is just fine. When you do find yourself feeling stable at level five, you're able to step up to the ladder's top rung. Look around. Savor your hard work. Stretch your arms out wide, close your eyes, and breathe in. As you take in the glorious view, ask yourself if you feel connected to something greater than yourself. Chances are, you do.

At this highest level, you desire a higher purpose. You want to help others move up the ladder. As educators, we're in luck here. In fact, it's probably why you chose this profession in the first place. You have a roster of students who you already help; during transcendence you can help in radical ways because your base is sturdy enough. Can you imagine a school where the adults in the building are so steady and solid that they regularly tap into this level? Imagine the impact this would have on the students lucky enough to be part of this environment.

Remember, this level is fleeting—unfortunately. No one arrives here, unpacks his or her bags, and stays for an extended time. Instead, you visit this space, just like you visit self-actualization. It may feel disappointing to know that you don't stay forever at level five or six. Consider, however, that your goals will evolve as you learn, providing opportunities to experience self-actualization. Being at these two levels is so transformational, allowing you to fully thrive, that it reinforces a need to get back to these levels as often as possible.

Self-actualization level needs are about fulfilling your *own* potential and finding your *own* happiness. Transcendence needs represent your broader perspective, whether that includes your students, community, or spirituality, and so on. Maslow (1969) relates this level to a feeling of connecting to the world in powerful ways, as though you are outside ordinary experience.

How can you reach this state amid the everyday chaos? Just like with all other levels, start by ensuring all the levels below it are solid. When you've done that, strive to be inspired and to help others (in particular, but not limited to, your students) on a regular basis. Specifically, you'll explore strategies related to seeking inspiration, practicing gratitude, and engaging in mindfulness and altruism, thus allowing you not only to lead a life of happiness yourself (self-actualization) but also to connect to something outside yourself (transcendence). These areas push us to look outside ourselves and focus on the world in different ways.

My mentor, researcher and author Robert J. Marzano, and his colleagues (2017) say, "inspiration occurs when people see evidence that one or more of their ideals could actually be true" (p. 12). As an example to get you started, I have an ideal that women are equal to men, and so I was extremely inspired to watch Hillary Clinton run for president of the United States in the 2016 election. I also have an ideal that people who work hard can achieve great things, so I love to hear public figures tell their rags-to-riches stories. I cry every time. I'm also drawn to books, especially memoirs, where someone shares his or her life and helps me see what it means to be a messy human being in a most beautiful way.

Before getting into the strategies, spend some time answering the following questions. They will help you reflect on your current transcendence and connection to the outside world.

What inspires you? Do these inspirations have similarities?

....

....

How does cultivating gratitude help you feel connected to something greater than yourself?

....

....

How does your body feel during mindfulness practices?

....

....

How do you practice compassion?

....

....

Transcendence Strategies

Inspiration is a quantifiable phenomenon. Researchers Todd Thrash and Andrew Elliot (2004) explain that you can split inspiration into two pieces: (1) being "inspired 'by'" something or someone, and (2) being "inspired 'to'" do or be something. They also assert, after studying, that people who experience inspiration daily are "high in receptive engagement," or open to new experiences. Inspiration doesn't just come to you—you either encounter or seek it.

The following sections have sample inspiration, gratitude, mindfulness, and altruism strategies to meet your transcendence needs on a regular basis. You can't do all of these starting today, but choose one or two that will be *most* helpful to you in the moments you *don't* feel connected to something greater than yourself. Refer to these strategies when you create your action plan in the next section.

Inspiration Strategies

Movies, books, and songs are a good starting place. Examples of books (adapted into movies) include *The Power of One* (Courtenay, 1996), *Hidden Figures* (Shetterly, 2016), and *Wild* (Strayed, 2013).

What top-five movies, books, or songs have stayed with you? Were they inspirational stories? What ideal and evidence did they provide to help you believe that ideal could be true?

....

....

Poignant quotes are another way to prompt inspiration. Many people, like me, collect quotes because they often state ideals. We can hold on to a quote and use it as a mantra for inspiration. Here are a few of my favorites (BrainyQuote, n.d.).

- "As we express our gratitude, we must never forget that the highest appreciation is not to utter words but to live by them." —John F. Kennedy

- "Change your thoughts and you change your world." — Norman Vincent Peale

- "What we think, we become." —Gautama Buddha

- "I can't change the direction of the wind, but I can adjust my sails to always reach my destination." —Jimmy Dean

- "We know what we are, but know not what we may be." —William Shakespeare

- "It is during our darkest moments that we must focus to see the light." —Aristotle Onassis

- "A hero is someone who has given his or her life to something bigger than oneself." —Joseph Campbell

- "My mission in life is not merely to survive, but to thrive; and to do so with some passion, some compassion, some humor, and some style." —Maya Angelou

Record your own favorite inspirational quotes here. (If you don't have any, visit https://values.com/inspirational-quotes to find some that resonate.)

- ....

- ....

Gratitude Strategies

Practicing gratitude is another way to help you connect to something greater than yourself. The notion of establishing a gratitude practice is popular (thanks, Oprah!), and science supports its benefits: "Gratitude is strongly and consistently associated with greater happiness. Gratitude helps people feel more positive emotions, relish good experiences, improve their health, deal with adversity, and build strong relationships" (Harvard Health Publishing, 2011). Booyah! Sign me up, right? Gratitude forces you to recognize something meaningful, and by doing that, you feel transcendent. You connect to something greater than yourself and to greater happiness.

To further illustrate this point, consider professors and researchers Robert A. Emmons and Michael E. McCullough's (2003) study. They asked participants, who they divided into three groups, to record a few sentences each week focusing on particular topics. One group recorded things they were grateful for during the week; a second group wrote about daily irritations or things that upset them; and a third group wrote about events that affected them (without emphasizing either positive or negative impact). The group that wrote about things they were grateful for reported feeling more optimistic and better about their lives. This group also exercised more and had fewer doctor visits than those in the other two groups.

Consider different ways that you can cultivate gratitude in your own life (Harvard Health Publishing, 2011).

- Write a thank-you note. I personally like traditional hard-copy thank-you notes over texts and emails. I also like to read the letter aloud to the recipient—bring tissue—and love the idea of writing one to yourself every once in a while.

- Thank someone mentally. Even if just in your mind, this is a positive thought running through your head in an otherwise somewhat negative world.

- Keep a gratitude journal. Write in your journal daily, weekly, or monthly. Experiment and decide what works best for you.

- Ask your family, colleagues, and students to engage in gratitude practices.

  o Have your family share what they're grateful for around the dinner table, in the car while running errands, or before bed.

  o Have students share what they're grateful for aloud or in writing, either publicly or privately, on a regular basis.

  o Start faculty, department, or grade-level meetings with gratitude statements.

  o Have paper and a drop box in the staff lounge (or somewhere in your home) where people can anonymously record their gratitude for others. Publish these posts every month either in a newsletter or verbally.

To get started, list here at least ten things for which you are grateful.

1. ....

2. ....

3. ....

4. ....

5. ....

6. ....

7. ....

8. ....

9. ....

10. ....

Mindfulness Strategies

Mindfulness is another way to help cultivate transcendence, because its many strategies can result in connecting powerfully to the world and feeling outside everyday existence. It took me a long time to embrace this idea; I saw it as a far-out quasi-psychological concept that I did *not* have time for. But darn it, it just kept popping up and getting my attention—through research (Carson, Carson, Gil, & Baucom, 2004; Hoge et al., 2013; Tang et al., 2007), articles, friends, and colleagues who mentioned the word *mindfulness* every time I turned around.

I finally tried it, and I hated it. I couldn't shut off my mind, and my ten minutes of silence felt like ten minutes of pure torture. So I quit for a while. Then I went back to it, but this time I was equipped with the app Headspace (https://headspace.com/headspace -meditation-app). I broke some rules and put on the meditation before I went to bed, but I'll tell you what—I fell asleep before the meditation was over—every single time—and slept like a baby. As a person who sometimes struggles to fall or stay asleep, this alone was a gift.

I stuck with it. I downloaded more apps and committed to mindfulness at least a few minutes each day, ideally in the morning before the chaos set in—and it worked. I began to feel a sense of calm that I hadn't felt in a long time. When I checked in with myself and discovered I was anxious or feeling out of control, deep mindful breaths soothed me and brought me back to reality, which was never as bad as what I perceived. Consider the following strategies to cultivate mindfulness in your own life.

- Use a meditation app a few days a week. Visit **go.SolutionTree.com/instruction** to access live links to some of my favorite meditation apps.

- Challenge yourself to sit in silence for at least five minutes every day.

- Go on a mindful walk. Be aware of each step and breath you take.

- Practice mindful listening. Be fully present when you're talking with someone.

- Try mindful eating. Remove all distractions and pay attention to how your food looks, feels, tastes, smells, and sounds while you're eating.

Record any other mindfulness strategies that you use or want to try.

- ....

- ....

Altruism Strategies

Altruism has different definitions depending on who you ask, but in this context, let's consider an *altruist* as "someone who does something for the other and for the other's sake, rather than as a means to self-promotion or internal well-being" (Post, 2002, p. 53).

Engaging in altruistic acts is an incredible way to feel connected to something bigger than yourself (Batson, 2011; Midlarsky & Kahana, 1994) and improve your well-being. Think about it: when we help others, we feel good. Research shows the "link between well-being and altruism may be particularly important in light of increased focus on policies that focus on societal level well-being, above and beyond economic well-being" (Marsh, 2014a). Consider the following strategies to cultivate altruism in your life.

- Be generous. Consider ways you can be generous with your time, attention, or money.

- Show kindness. Do so with everyone you meet. Create your own definition of kindness and work on being an ambassador of kindness every single day.

- Show compassion. Be empathic toward others. Consider someone else's perspective and how it feels to be in his or her shoes.

- Try volunteering. Find local organizations that need help (start at www.volunteermatch.org). What causes are most important to you? Find out how you can help (Li & Ferraro, 2005; Thoits & Hewitt, 2001).

Record any other transcendence strategies that you use or want to try.

- ....

- ....

Considering all of these transcendence strategies—inspiration, gratitude, mindfulness, and altruism—I decided to use the following strategies.

- I meditate for at least five minutes a day using an app like Headspace.

- I have a gratitude log as part of my planner, and I share my gratitude through social media.

- I collect inspirational quotes.

- I send personal thank-you notes.

- I volunteer with a student writing organization in my hometown once a month.

- I give money to charities that are important to me.

- I strive to be kind toward everyone I meet every day by smiling at strangers and holding doors for others.

Now that I've shared some of my go-to strategies, it's time to think about your own level six action plan and which strategies you want to focus on this week.

My Level Six Action Plan: Transcendence Needs

You can create your own action plan for this level, similar to what I did for myself.

1. Go back and circle all the strategies in this chapter that appeal to you, including those you may have added on your own. At this point, don't worry about how many you're selecting; simply choose any that sound good to you and record them in the space following. You can list the strategies exactly as I described them earlier or you can tap into your creative side by including pictures or doodles or finding photos online that represent the strategies.

   ....

   ....

   ....

2. Now narrow down your selected strategies to a reasonable number. Only you can determine what feels reasonable to you. Consider how much work each strategy entails, what your daily schedule looks like right now, and whether you want to choose strategies that feel easy or you want to choose ones that stretch you. List your selected reasonable number of strategies in figure 7.1 (pages 110 and 111).

3. Decide which days you plan to employ each strategy, putting a check mark under those days in the Goal row. If you are working with an accountability partner or group, answer the questions at the end of the action plan as well.

4. Keep your action plan with you for the next seven days. Track which days you employ your chosen strategies and make any notes you'd like. For example, you might record how different you felt after using the strategy, or that the strategy doesn't seem to have an impact yet. Keep your notes simple, so tracking stays manageable.

At week's end, answer the reflection questions on page 112 or 114.

Week _____

Strategy	Sunday	Monday	Tuesday	Wednesday	Thursday	Friday	Saturday
Goal							
Actual							
Notes:							
Goal							
Actual							
Notes:							
Goal							
Actual							
Notes:							

Goal					
Actual					
Notes:					
Goal					
Actual					
Notes:					

If you're working with an accountability partner or group:

How can your partner or group help with your accountability? (For example, can you check in with one another daily via text, via email, or face-to-face?) List your ideas here.

How can you help support your accountability partner or group? List your ideas here.

Source: Adapted from Mind Tools Content Team, n.d.a.

FIGURE 7.1: MY TRANSCENDENCE ACTION PLAN.

Visit go.SolutionTree.com/instruction for a free reproducible version of this figure.

Reflection Questions

After following your action plan for one week and utilizing your selected strategies, respond to the following questions to determine if they positively impacted your life and whether you need to stay at this level for another week or if you're ready to move to the next level.

What worked well for you this week? Why?

—— •●• ——

Where did you struggle? Why?

—— •●• ——

Did you use the selected strategies on the intended days? If so, how did that impact you? If not, why not? (Was it an issue of time, perhaps? Did something unexpected happen to you this week?)

—— •●• ——

What differences do you notice in how you feel throughout the day after implementing your strategies?

—— •●• ——

As you think ahead to next week, would it be helpful to stay at this level and either (1) engage in the same strategies again or (2) select different strategies to work on? Or is it time to move to the next level? How do you know?

—— •●• ——

As an educator, how does focusing on your own transcendence needs impact your work at school? As a person, how does focusing on your own transcendence needs impact your life outside of school?

—— •●• ——

Record any other thoughts related to your transcendence needs strategies.

— NOTES —

Reflection Questions
for Accountability Partners and Groups

Before meeting with your accountability partner or group, reflect on the following questions alone. When you meet with your accountability partner or group, have each person share his or her completed action plan, notes, and responses to the individual and group reflection questions.

How did working with a partner or a group help you this week?

—— •●• ——

What could your partner or group have done to help you in areas you struggled?

—— •●• ——

What kind of support would you like from your partner or group in the coming weeks, and how can you ensure that happens?

—— •●• ——

What did you do to help your partner or others in your group?

—— •●• ——

What can you do to help your partner or others in your
group that you didn't do this week?

— Notes —

EPILOGUE
Final Thoughts

At my annual checkup, my doctor noticed that I had worked to make some serious life changes that positively impacted my overall health. My weight was down, my skin was clear, and my blood pressure was ideal. I beamed with pride. Since I'd seen her the year before, I had revamped my life and was no longer suffering from exhaustion, stress, low self-esteem, and mild anxiety. I walked my talk and did the things I've asked you to do in this book. My hope is that after trying to meet the needs every human has, you're feeling exactly as I did—amazing. I hope someone else in your life (in addition to me) will congratulate you for living life as your best self. (You're in luck if you're working with an accountability partner or group!)

In the following sections, you get to celebrate just how far you've come.

Self-Care Survey: Growth Check

For each statement, check the box in figure E.1 that reflects the frequency of your behavior within the past seven days.

In the past week, how many days did you do the following?	Never (zero days)	Rarely (one day)	Sometimes (two to three days)	Often (four to five days)	Always (six to seven days)
Physiology					
I drank at least six glasses of water.					
I got at least seven hours of sleep.					
I ate a variety of nutritious foods from a range of food groups.					
I engaged in physical activity.					
Safety					
I felt safe at school.					
I felt safe at home or away from school.					
I felt a sense of order or consistency at school.					
I felt a sense of order or consistency at home or away from school.					
Belonging					
I felt included and respected at school.					
I felt included and respected at home or away from school.					
I felt like a coworker truly cared about my well-being.					
I felt like a family member or friend truly cared about my well-being.					

Esteem					
I spoke kindly to myself.					
I felt competent in my job.					
I felt important at home or school.					
Someone recognized the work I do at school or elsewhere.					
Self-Actualization					
I set personal goals at home or school.					
I believed I could accomplish what I set out to do.					
I had a positive outlook on the future at home or school.					
I had a moment of flow or a peak experience (where I felt totally, completely happy and at peace) at home or school.					
Transcendence					
I felt inspired at home or at school.					
I did something at home or at school for someone else without anyone asking me to.					
I felt empathy toward someone else or I forgave someone at home or at school.					
I felt a sense of gratitude or engaged in mindfulness.					

FIGURE E.1: SELF-CARE SURVEY: GROWTH CHECK.

*Visit **go.SolutionTree.com/instruction** for a free reproducible version of this figure.*

After taking your self-care survey and checking for growth, reflect on and respond to the following questions.

How did it feel to take the survey this time?

....

....

Were you surprised by the results? In what way?

....

....

In what area are you thriving the most? How does this make you feel?

....

....

In what area are you the most challenged? How does this make you feel?

....

....

Would the results have been different during other times of your life (for better or for worse)?

....

....

What areas do you want to focus on the most? Why?

....

....

If you could change one thing in your life as a result of reflecting on your survey, what would it be and why?

....

....

Daily Time Audit: Growth Check

Use the "Daily Time Audit: Growth Check" (figure E.2) to determine where you're spending the majority of your day and the value of each activity in your life. During an entire day, record every activity's start and end times. Briefly describe what you're doing, how you feel while engaged in the activity, and how highly you value it.

Start and End Times	Activity Description	How I Feel	Value (High, Medium, Low, Neutral)

Source: Adapted from Mind Tools Content Team, n.d.b.

FIGURE E.2: DAILY TIME AUDIT: GROWTH CHECK.

*Visit **go.SolutionTree.com/instruction** for a free reproducible version of this figure.*

Once you've recorded a few days (again, capture a typical work-day and a typical weekend day), reflect on these questions.

How much time are you spending on low-value tasks versus high-value tasks? How has this shifted from the first time you conducted your audit?

....

....

When are you most energized? When are you the least energized? What changes have you made since conducting your first audit?

....

....

What contributes to your positive emotions? What activities make you feel negative emotions?

....

....

How are your feelings related to your values now?

....

....

How is your "Daily Time Audit: Growth Check" different for a weekday and a weekend day? Is this different from the first time you analyzed your time?

....

....

Now that you've had time to celebrate your own new habits and positive changes in your life, I invite you to work through the appendix (page 123), where you'll create your own targeted master self-care plan, which will work as your personal blueprint for self-care.

My greatest hope is that you are now living your best life, as both an educator and a human being, and that you feel the gift of connecting to something greater than yourself. Thank you for taking the time to secure your own oxygen mask first. This might be the single greatest gift you've ever given to yourself or those you love. Go live your very best life as an educator *and* a human being. Continue working to meet your needs and strive to fully thrive. I am cheering you on!

APPENDIX

My Personalized Self-Care Plan

By now, I hope you have a better sense of yourself and recognize when you're merely surviving versus when you're truly thriving. I also hope that when you are not your best self, you know that you have a slew of strategies, depending on what you need in that moment. In fact, now that you've had time to practice and reflect, it's time to create a *cheat sheet*—a quick-reference guide—to carry with you and refer to on a daily or regular basis. This will be your personalized "Self-Care Plan" (page 124). To complete your plan, take time to review and reflect on the previous chapters and identify the strategies that seem to work best for you. In your "Self-Care Plan," record those strategies in a way that makes sense to you. I suggest making multiple copies of this and putting them in the same places you first posted the framework questions (see figure 1.4, page 19).

Self-Care Plan

Identify the self-care strategies that seem to work best for you.

Level and Need	Ask Yourself	Go-To Strategies
Level one: Physiology	Are my basic needs met?	
Level two: Safety	Do I feel safe?	
Level three: Belonging	Do I feel like I belong?	
Level four: Esteem	Do I feel confident?	
Level five: Self-Actualization	Am I living my best life?	
Level six: Transcendence	Do I feel connected to something greater than myself?	

REFERENCES AND RESOURCES

20 tips for better sleep [Slide show]. (2016, October 6). Accessed at https://webmd
.com/a-to-z-guides/discomfort-15/better-sleep/slideshow-sleep-tips on October
10, 2017.

Alban, D. (n.d.). *12 effects of chronic stress on your brain.* Accessed at https://bebrainfit
.com/effects-chronic-stress-brain on December 16, 2016.

American Psychological Association. (n.d.). *Five tips to help manage stress.* Accessed at
www.apa.org/helpcenter/manage-stress.aspx on November 10, 2017.

Babauta, L. (2008, June 29). *9 steps to achieving flow (and happiness) in your work* [Blog
post]. Accessed at https://zenhabits.net/guide-to-achieving-flow-and-happiness
-in-your-work on March 5, 2018.

Barnet, T. (n.d.). *Motivation and motivation theory.* Accessed at www.referenceforbusiness
.com/management/Mar-No/Motivation-and-Motivation-Theory.html on
December 16, 2016.

Batson, C. D. (2011). *Altruism in humans.* New York: Oxford University Press.

Baumeister, R. F., & Leary, M. R. (1995). The need to belong: Desire for
interpersonal attachments as a fundamental human motivation. *Psychological
Bulletin, 117*(3), 497–529.

Bearman, P. S., & Moody, J. (2004, January). Suicide and friendships among
American adolescents. *American Journal of Public Health, 94*(1), 89–95.

Beck, A. T. (1993). Cognitive therapy: Past, present, and future. *Journal of Consulting
and Clinical Psychology, 61*(2), 194–198.

Beck, J. S. (1995). *Cognitive therapy: Basics and beyond.* New York: Guilford Press.

Beetz, A., Uvnäs-Moberg, K., Julius, H., & Kotrschal, K. (2012, July 9). Psychosocial and psychophysiological effects of human-animal interactions: The possible role of oxytocin. *Frontiers in Psychology.* Accessed at www.frontiersin.org /articles/10.3389/fpsyg.2012.00234/full on February 28, 2018.

Bernhard, T. (2014, September 29). How distorted thinking increases stress and anxiety. *Psychology Today.* Accessed at www.psychologytoday.com/blog/turning -straw-gold/201409/how-distorted-thinking-increases-stress-and-anxiety on March 5, 2018.

Blanchard, K. (2007). *Leading at a higher level: Blanchard on leadership and creating high performing organizations.* Upper Saddle River, NJ: Prentice Hall.

Bohn, J. (2014, October 20). *The importance of base camp for career climbers.* Accessed at https://linkedin.com/pulse/20141020213323-11890051-the-importance-of -base-camp-for-career-climbers on December 16, 2016.

Bonci, L. (2009, February 1). *What does "shop the perimeter" mean?* Accessed at http:// abcnews.go.com/Health/WellnessResource/story?id=6762968 on November 7, 2017.

Boogren, T. H. (2012, January 1). *The dialectical-level reflective habits of middle- grade teachers: A phenomenological study* (Unpublished dissertation). University of Denver, Colorado. Accessed at https://digitalcommons.du.edu/cgi/viewcontent .cgi?article=1764&context=etd on February 26, 2018.

Boogren, T. H. (2015). *Supporting beginning teachers.* Bloomington, IN: Marzano Research.

BrainyQuote. (n.d.). *Home.* Accessed at https://brainyquote.com on December 16, 2016.

Brown, B. (n.d.). *Brené Brown's top 4 life lessons.* Accessed at www.oprah.com/spirit /Life-Lessons-We-All-Need-to-Learn-Brene-Brown on December 16, 2016.

Brown, B. B., & Larson, J. (2009). 3 peer relationships in adolescence. In R. M. Lerner & L. Steinberg (Eds.), *Handbook of adolescent psychology, volume 2: Contextual influences on adolescent development* (3rd ed., pp. 74–103). Hoboken, NJ: Wiley.

Bubb, S., & Earley, P. (2004). *Managing teacher workload: Work-life balance and wellbeing.* London: Chapman.

Buddha, G. (n.d.). *Quote.* Accessed at www.goodreads.com/quotes/984978-if-you -want-to-know-your-past-life-look-at on February 26, 2018.

Burns, D. D. (2008). *Feeling good: The new mood therapy.* New York: Harper.

Bushman, B. J., DeWall, C. N., Pond, R. S., Jr., & Hanus, M. D. (2014). Low glucose relates to greater aggression in married couples. *Proceedings of the National Academy of Sciences of the United States of America, 111*(17), 6254–6257.

BusyTeacher.org. (n.d.). *Home.* Accessed at https://busyteacher.org/16670-teachers -masters-of-multitasking-infographic.html on February 26, 2018.

Cacioppo, J. T., & Hawkley, L. C. (2009). Loneliness. In M. R. Leary & R. H. Hoyle (Eds.), *Handbook of individual differences in social behavior* (pp. 227–240). New York: Guilford Press.

Capretto, L. (2014, February 25). *Brené Brown on self-criticism, judgment and the power of compassion.* Accessed at www.huffingtonpost.com/2014/02/25/brene -brown-self-criticism-compassion_n_4848895.html on December 16, 2016.

Cardwell, M. E. (2011, August). *Patterns of relationships between teacher engagement and student engagement* (Unpublished doctoral dissertation). St. John Fisher College, Rochester, New York. Accessed at https://fisherpub.sjfc.edu/cgi/viewcontent .cgi?referer=https://www.google.com/&httpsredir=1&article=1050&context =education_etd on November 28, 2017.

Carson, J. W., Carson, K. M., Gil, K. M., & Baucom, D. H. (2004). Mindfulness-based relationship enhancement. *Behavior Therapy, 35*(3), 471–494.

Carter, E., & Watts, P. (2016, January 22). *The science of hunger and what makes us "hangry."* Accessed at www.independent.co.uk/life-style/health-and-families /features/the-science-of-hunger-and-what-makes-us-hangry-a6828111.html on February 28, 2018.

Cascio, C. N., O'Donnell, M. B., Tinney, F. J., Lieberman, M. D., Taylor, S. E., Strecher, V. J., et al. (2016). Self-affirmation activates brain systems associated with self-related processing and reward and is reinforced by future orientation. *Social Cognitive and Affective Neuroscience, 11*(4), 621–629.

Centers for Disease Control and Prevention. (2015). *Insufficient sleep is a public health problem.* Accessed at https://cdc.gov/features/dssleep/index.html#References on November 30, 2017.

Cherry, K. (2016, May 10). *What are peak experiences?* [Blog post]. Accessed at https://verywell.com/what-are-peak-experiences-2795268 on December 16, 2016.

Cook-Cottone, C. P. (2015). *Mindfulness and yoga for self-regulation: A primer for mental health professionals.* New York: Springer.

Courtenay, B. (1996). *The power of one: A novel.* New York: Ballantine.

Crocker, J. (2002). The costs of seeking self-esteem. *Journal of Social Issues*, *58*(3), 597–615.

Csikszentmihalyi, M. (1990). *Flow: The psychology of optimal experience*. New York: Harper & Row.

Csikszentmihalyi, M. (2008). *Flow: The psychology of optimal experience*. New York: Harper Perennial.

Csikszentmihalyi, M., & Csikszentmihalyi, I. S. (Eds.). (1988). *Optimal experience: Psychological studies of flow in consciousness*. Cambridge, England: Cambridge University Press.

Devine, M. (2013, December 11). *The 5 stages of grief and other lies that don't help anyone* [Blog post]. Accessed at www.huffingtonpost.com/megan-devine/stages -of-grief_b_4414077.html on November 13, 2017.

de Zwaan, M., Burgard, M. A., Schenck, C. H., & Mitchell, J. E. (2003). Night time eating: A review of the literature. *European Eating Disorders Review*, *11*, 7–24.

Divine, M. (2017, September 21). *How goal setting helps reduce stress*. Accessed at https://unbeatablemind.com/how-goal-setting-helps-reduce-stress on March 5, 2018.

Doran, G. T. (1981). There's a S.M.A.R.T. way to write management's goals and objectives. *Management Review*, *70*(11), 35–36.

Drake, C., Roehrs, T., Shambroom, J., & Roth, T. (2013). Caffeine effects on sleep taken 0, 3, or 6 hours before going to bed. *Journal of Clinical Sleep Medicine*, *9*(11), 1195–2000. Accessed at https://ncbi.nlm.nih.gov/pubmed/24235903 on November 8, 2017.

Dweck, C. S. (2006). *Mindset: The new psychology of success*. New York: Random House.

Emmons, R. A., & McCullough, M. E. (2003). Counting blessings versus burdens: An experimental investigation of gratitude and subjective well-being in daily life. *Journal of Personality and Social Psychology*, *84*(2), 377–389.

Francis, M. (2005, January 15). *Hangry*. Accessed at www.urbandictionary.com /define.php?term=Hangry on November 7, 2017.

Friedman, I. A. (2000). Burnout in teachers: Shattered dreams of impeccable professional performance. *Journal of Clinical Psychology*, *56*(5), 595–606. Accessed at http://curriculumstudies.pbworks.com/f/Burnout+in+Teachers+ -+Isaac+Friedman.pdf on November 14, 2017.

Gardner, B., Lally, P., & Wardle, J. (2012). Making health habitual: The psychology of 'habit-formation' and general practice. *British Journal of General Practice*, *62*(605), 664–666. Accessed at www.ncbi.nlm.nih.gov/pmc/articles/PMC3505409/#b3 on April 6, 2018.

Gigliotti, D., Chernin, P., Topping, J., Williams, P., & Melfi, T. (Producers), & Melfi, T. (Director). (2016). *Hidden figures* [Motion picture]. United States: 20th Century Fox.

Glass, L. (2015). *Toxic people: 10 ways of dealing with people who make your life miserable.* Beverly Hills, CA: Your Total Image.

Gooley, J. J., Chamberlain, K., Smith, K. A., Khalsa, S. B., Rajaratnam, S. M., Van Reen, E., et al. (2011). Exposure to room light before bedtime suppresses melatonin onset and shortens melatonin duration in humans. *The Journal of Clinical Endocrinology and Metabolism*, *96*(3), E463–E472.

Gregoire, C. (2013, August 11). *The 75-year study that found the secrets to a fulfilling life.* Accessed at www.huffingtonpost.com/2013/08/11/how-this-harvard -psycholo_n_3727229.html on December 4, 2017.

Gunuc, S. (2014, October). The relationships between student engagement and their academic achievement. *International Journal on New Trends in Education and Their Implications*, *5*(4). Accessed at www.ijonte.org/FileUpload/ks63207 /File/19..gunuc.pdf on November 28, 2017.

Harrill, S. E. (n.d.). *Self-worth: Recognizing signs of high and low self-esteem.* Accessed at www.innerworkspublishing.com/news/vol40/selfesteem.htm on October 10, 2017.

Harvard Health Publishing. (2011, November). *In praise of gratitude.* Accessed at https://health.harvard.edu/newsletter_article/in-praise-of-gratitude on December 16, 2016.

Harvard Health Publishing. (2015, September 2). *Blue light has a dark side.* Accessed at https://health.harvard.edu/staying-healthy/blue-light-has-a-dark-side on September 3, 2017.

Haze, S., Sakai, K., & Gozu, Y. (2002). Effects of fragrance inhalation on sympathetic activity in normal adults. *The Japanese Journal of Pharmacology*, *90*(3), 247–253.

Henry, S. K. (2012). On social connection in university life. *About Campus*, *16*(6), 18–24.

Herzberg, F. (2008). *Frederick Herzberg papers.* Accessed at http://archiveswest .orbiscascade.org/ark:/80444/xv73168 on November 27, 2017.

Hoge, E. A., Bui, E., Marques, L., Metcalf, C. A., Morris, L. K., Robinaugh, D. J., et al. (2013). Randomized controlled trial of mindfulness meditation for generalized anxiety disorder: Effects on anxiety and stress reactivity. *Journal of Clinical Psychiatry, 74*(8), 786–792.

Holmes, L. (2014, May 20). *How anxiety influences your health.* Accessed at www .huffingtonpost.com/2014/05/20/your-body-on-anxiety_n_5352548.html on December 1, 2017.

Huffington, A. (2016). *The sleep revolution: Transforming your life, one night at a time.* New York: Harmony Books.

Ingersoll, R. M. (2012, May 16). Beginning teacher induction: What the data tell us. *Education Week.* Accessed at www.edweek.org/ew/articles/2012/05/16/kappan _ingersoll.h31.html on January 2, 2018.

Jarrett, C. (2015, November 16). *Brain scans can help explain why self-affirmation works.* Accessed at http://nymag.com/scienceofus/2015/11/why-self-affirmation -works.html on November 14, 2017.

Joseph, S. (2016, September 13). *What is self-actualization?* [Blog post]. Accessed at https://psychologytoday.com/blog/what-doesnt-kill-us/201609/what-is-self -actualization on October 10, 2017.

Keys, A., Brožek, J., Henschel, A., Mickelson, O., & Taylor, H. L. (1950). *The biology of human starvation, volumes 1–2.* Minneapolis, MN: University of Minnesota Press.

Lebowitz, S. (2015, June 1). *How to actually get sh!t done with a to-do list.* Accessed at https://greatist.com/happiness/make-a-to-do-list-get-shit-done on December 16, 2016.

LeWine, H. (2013, March 29). *Distracted eating may add to weight gain* [Blog post]. Accessed at https://health.harvard.edu/blog/distracted-eating-may-add-to -weight-gain-201303296037 on November 7, 2017.

Li, Y., & Ferraro, K. F. (2005). Volunteering and depression in later life: Social benefit or selection processes? *Journal of Health and Social Behavior, 46*(1), 68–84.

Lovato, N., & Lack, L. (2010). The effects of napping on cognitive functioning. *Progress in Brain Research, 185*, 155–166.

Maclay, K. (2016, June 15). *A Berkeley expert assesses personal security in an on-edge America.* Accessed at http://news.berkeley.edu/2016/06/15/a-berkeley-expert -assesses-personal-security-in-an-on-edge-america on November 10, 2017.

Marsh, A. (2014a, January 29). *Altruistic acts more common in states with high well-being.* Accessed at https://psychologicalscience.org/news/releases/altruistic -acts-more-common-in-states-with-high-well-being.html#.WW0ugcaZOqA on October 10, 2017.

Marsh, S. (2014b, November 20). *Daily tips to help teachers stay happy and healthy during the week* [Blog post]. Accessed at https://theguardian.com/teacher -network/teacher-blog/2014/nov/20/tips-teachers-happy-healthy-week on December 16, 2016.

Marzano, R. J., Scott, D., Boogren, T. H., & Newcomb, M. L. (2017). *Motivating & inspiring students: Strategies to awaken the learner.* Bloomington, IN: Marzano Research.

Marzano Research. (n.d.). *The Marzano Compendium of Instructional Strategies.* Accessed at www.marzanoresearch.com/online-compendium on December 16, 2016.

Maslow, A. H. (1943). A theory of human motivation. *Psychological Review, 50*(4), 370–396.

Maslow, A. H. (1954). *Motivation and personality.* New York: Harper.

Maslow, A. H. (1969). The farther reaches of human nature. *Journal of Transpersonal Psychology, 1*(1), 1–9.

Maslow, A. H. (1971). *The farther reaches of human nature.* New York: Viking Press.

Maslow, A. H. (2000). *The Maslow business reader.* New York: Wiley.

Maslow, A. H. (2013). *A theory of human motivation.* Eastford, CT: Martino Fine Books. (Original work published 1943)

Maslow, A. H. (2015). *Toward a psychology of being* (3rd ed.) [Kindle version]. Accessed at Amazon.com.

Mathur, P. (2011). Hand hygiene: Back to the basics of infection control. *Indian Journal of Medical Research, 134*(5), 611–620.

Mayo Clinic Staff. (n.d.). *Water: How much should you drink every day?* Accessed at www.mayoclinic.org/healthy-lifestyle/nutrition-and-healthy-eating/in-depth /water/art-20044256 on February 28, 2018.

Mayo Clinic Staff. (2016, October 13). *Exercise: 7 benefits of regular physical activity.* Accessed at www.mayoclinic.org/healthy-lifestyle/fitness/in-depth/exercise/art -20048389 on November 15, 2017.

McLeod, S. A. (2008). *Self concept.* Accessed at www.simplypsychology.org/self -concept.html on December 16, 2016.

McMahon, S. D., Espelage, D., Anderman, E. M., Lane, K. L., Reddy, L., Reynolds, C., et al. (2011). *National survey of violence against teachers: APA classroom violence directed against teachers task force report.* Washington, DC: American Psychological Association Board of Educational Affairs.

Melton, G. D. (2016). *Love warrior.* New York: Flatiron Books.

Midlarsky, E., & Kahana, E. (1994). *Altruism in later life.* Thousand Oaks, CA: SAGE.

Midlarsky, E. R., & Midlarsky, M. I. (2004). Echoes of genocide: Trauma and ethnic identity among European immigrants. *Humboldt Journal of Social Relations, 28*(2), 38–53.

Milchon, A. (Producer), & Avildsen, J. G. (Director). (1992). *The power of one* [Motion picture]. United States: Warner Brothers.

Mind Tools Content Team. (n.d.a). *Action plans: Small-scale planning.* Accessed at https://mindtools.com/pages/article/newHTE_04.htm on December 16, 2016.

Mind Tools Content Team. (n.d.b). *Activity logs: Finding more time in your day.* Accessed at https://mindtools.com/pages/article/newHTE_03.htm on December 16, 2016.

Mohr, T. (2014). *Playing big: Find your voice, your mission, your message.* New York: Gotham Books.

Morin, A. (2016, June 15). This is how your thoughts become your reality. *Forbes.* Accessed at www.forbes.com/sites/amymorin/2016/06/15/this-is-how-your -thoughts-become-your-reality/#42c62e5b528a on March 5, 2018.

Moser, J. S., Dougherty, A., Mattson, W. I., Katz, B., Moran, T. P., Guevarra, D., et al. (2017). Third-person self-talk facilitates emotion regulation without engaging cognitive control: Converging evidence from ERP and fMRI. *Scientific Reports, 7*(1), 4519.

Myllymäki, T., Kyröläinen, H., Savolainen, K., Hokka, L., Jakonen, R., Juuti, T., et al. (2011, March 20). Effects of vigorous late-night exercise on sleep quality and cardiac autonomic activity [Abstract]. *Journal of Sleep Research.* Accessed at https://ncbi.nlm.nih.gov/pubmed/20673290 on November 8, 2017.

Nair, R., & Maseeh, A. (2012). Vitamin D: The "sunshine" vitamin. *Journal of Pharmacology and Pharmacotherapeutics, 3*(2), 118–126.

Neff, K. (2011). *Self-compassion: Stop beating yourself up and leave insecurity behind.* New York: Morrow.

Newsome, B. (2015, November 18). *Surviving new terrorist attacks in 10 steps* [Blog post]. Accessed at http://blogs.berkeley.edu/2015/11/18/surviving-new -terrorism-in-10-steps on December 13, 2017.

Nezlek, J. B., Vansteelandt, K., Van Mechelen, I., & Kuppens, P. (2008). Appraisal-emotion relationships in daily life. *Emotion, 8*(1), 145–150.

Novak, J. M., & Purkey, W. W. (2001). *Invitational education.* Bloomington, IN: Phi Delta Kappa Educational Foundation.

O'Brien, M. (2014). *How to enter the "flow state" any time: 4 simple steps.* Accessed at https://mrsmindfulness.com/how-you-can-enter-mindfulness-in-4-simple-steps on October 10, 2017.

O'Neill, J., & Conzemius, A. (2006). *The power of SMART goals: Using goals to improve student learning.* Bloomington, IN: Solution Tree Press.

Oppland, M. (2016, December 16). Mihaly Csikszentmihalyi: All about flow and positive psychology. *Positive Psychology Program.* Accessed at https:// positivepsychologyprogram.com/mihaly-csikszentmihalyi-father-of-flow on October 10, 2017.

Peri, C. (2014). *10 things to hate about sleep loss.* Accessed at https://webmd.com /sleep-disorders/features/10-results-sleep-loss#1 on October 10, 2017.

Pickering, A. J., Boehm, A. B., Mwanjali, M., & Davis, J. (2010). Efficacy of waterless hand hygiene compared with handwashing with soap: A field study in Dar es Salaam, Tanzania. *The American Journal of Tropical Medicine and Hygiene, 82*(2), 270–278.

Post, S. G. (2002). The tradition of agape. In S. G. Post, L. G. Underwood, J. P. Schloss, & W. B. Hurlbut (Eds.), *Altruism and altruistic love: Science, philosophy, and religion in dialogue* (pp. 51–64). New York: Oxford University Press.

Pursuit of Happiness. (n.d.). *Abraham Maslow.* Accessed at www.pursuit-of -happiness.org/history-of-happiness/abraham-maslow on November 15, 2017.

Rath, T., & Clifton, D. O. (2007). *How full is your bucket? Educator's edition: Positive strategies for work and life.* New York: Gallup Press.

Richman, L. S., & Leary, M. R. (2009). Reactions to discrimination, stigmatization, ostracism, and other forms of interpersonal rejection: A multimotive model. *Psychological Review, 116*(2), 365–383.

Riggs, L. (2013, October 18). *Why do teachers quit? And why do they stay?* Accessed at https://theatlantic.com/education/archive/2013/10/why-do-teachers-quit /280699 on July 31, 2017.

Robers, S., Zhang, A., Morgan, R. E., & Musu-Gillette, L. (2015). *Indicators of school crime and safety: 2014.* Washington, DC: National Center for Education Statistics, U.S. Department of Education, and Bureau of Justice Statistics, Office of Justice Programs, U.S. Department of Justice. Accessed at http://nces.ed.gov/pubsearch/pubsinfo.asp?pubid=2015072 on December 16, 2016.

Rosen, L. D. (2012, April 9). *Attention alert! Study on distraction reveals some surprises.* Accessed at www.psychologytoday.com/blog/rewired-the-psychology-technology/201204/attention-alert-study-distraction-reveals-some on November 13, 2017.

Rumi, J. (n.d.). *Divan-e shams-e tabrizi.*

Safety. (n.d.). In *Dictionary.com.* Accessed at www.dictionary.com/browse/safety?s=t on October 10, 2017.

Sahoo, F. M., & Sahu, R. (2009). The role of flow experience in human happiness. *Journal of the Indian Academy of Applied Psychology, 35*(Special issue), 40–47.

Schoenborn, C. A., & Adams, P. F. (2010). Health behaviors of adults: United States, 2005–2007. *Vital and Health Statistics, 10*(245), 1–132.

School Improvement Network. (2013, January 23). *Guns and school safety survey results.* Accessed at http://schoolimprovement.com/voe/guns-and-school-safety-survey-results/?pr=guns-sinet on March 6, 2018.

Schwartz, M. (2010, February 17). *Self-esteem or other-esteem? What's the difference between self-esteem and other-esteem?* [Blog post]. Accessed at https://psychologytoday.com/blog/shift-mind/201002/self-esteem-or-other-esteem on October 10, 2017.

Shead, M. (n.d.). *How to do a time audit* [Blog post]. Accessed at www.productivity501.com/how-to-do-a-time-audit/7043 on December 16, 2016.

Shetterly, M. L. (2016). *Hidden figures: The American dream and the untold story of the black women mathematicians who helped win the space race.* New York: Morrow.

Smith, C., Hancock, H., Blake-Mortimer, J., & Eckert, K. (2007). A randomised comparative trial of yoga and relaxation to reduce stress and anxiety. *Complementary Therapies in Medicine, 15*(2), 77–83.

Southwick, S. M., & Charney, D. S. (2012). *Resilience: The science of mastering life's greatest challenges.* Cambridge, England: Cambridge University Press.

Sowislo, J. F., & Orth, U. (2013). Does low self-esteem predict depression and anxiety? A meta-analysis of longitudinal studies. *Psychological Bulletin, 139*(1), 213–240.

Stangor, C. (2014). *Principles of social psychology—1st international edition*. Boston: FlatWorld. Accessed at https://opentextbc.ca/socialpsychology/chapter/the -feeling-self-self-esteem on November 13, 2017.

Steiner-Adair, C., & Barker, T. H. (2013). *The big disconnect: Protecting childhood and family relationships in the digital age*. New York: HarperCollins.

Strayed, C. (2013). *Wild: From lost to found on the Pacific Crest Trail*. New York: Vintage Books.

Sze, D. (2015, July 21). *Maslow: The 12 characteristics of a self-actualized person*. Accessed at www.huffingtonpost.com/david-sze/maslow-the-12-characteris_b_7836836 .html on October 10, 2017.

Tang, Y. Y., Ma, Y., Wang, J., Fan, Y., Feng, S., Lu, Q., et al. (2007). Short-term meditation training improves attention and self-regulation. *Proceedings of the National Academy of Sciences of the United States of America, 104*(43), 17152–17156.

Thoits, P. A., & Hewitt, L. N. (2001). Volunteer work and well-being. *Journal of Health and Social Behavior, 42*(2), 115–131.

Thoma, M. V., La Marca, R., Brönnimann, R., Finkel, L., Ehlert, U., & Nater, U. M. (2013). The effect of music on the human stress response. *PLOS One, 8*(8).

Thomas, S. (n.d.). *Maslow's safety needs: Examples and definition* [Video and lesson transcript]. Accessed at http://study.com/academy/lesson/maslows-safety-needs -examples-definition-quiz.html on December 16, 2016.

Thompson, E. G., & O'Brien, R. (2014). *Symptoms of low blood sugar—topic overview*. Accessed at https://webmd.com/a-to-z-guides/tc/symptoms-of-low -blood-sugar-topic-overview on November 7, 2017.

Thrash, T. M., & Elliot, A. J. (2004, December). Inspiration: Core characteristics, component processes, antecedents, and function [Abstract]. *Journal of Personality and Social Psychology, 87*(6), 957–973.

Toda, M., & Morimoto, K. (2008). Effect of lavender aroma on salivary endocrinological stress markers. *Archives of Oral Biology, 53*(10), 964–968.

Toppo, G. (2013, November 13). *Schools safe as ever despite spate of shootings, scares*. Accessed at https://usatoday.com/story/news/nation/2013/11/13/school -violence-security-sandy-hook/3446023 on October 10, 2017.

Tschannen-Moran, M., & Hoy, W. (1998). Trust in schools: A conceptual and empirical analysis. *Journal of Educational Administration, 36*(4), 334–352. Accessed at www.researchgate.net/publication/235295498_A_Conceptual_and _Empirical_Analysis_of_Trust_in_Schools on October 19, 2017.

Tudor-Locke, C., & Bassett, D. R., Jr. (2004). How many steps/day are enough? Preliminary pedometer indices for public health. *Sports Medicine, 34*(1), 1–8.

Ullrich, P. M., & Lutgendorf, S. K. (2002). Journaling about stressful events: Effects of cognitive processing and emotional expression. *Annals of Behavioral Medicine, 24*(3), 244–250.

Uvnäs-Moberg, K. (2003). *The oxytocin factor: Tapping the hormone of calm, love, and healing* (R. Francis, Trans.). Boston: Da Capo Press.

Vaillant, G. E. (2012). *Triumphs of experience: The men of the Harvard Grant Study.* Cambridge, MA: Harvard University Press.

Vartanian, L. R., Schwartz, M. B., & Brownell, K. D. (2007). Effects of soft drink consumption on nutrition and health: A systematic review and meta-analysis. *American Journal of Public Health, 97*(4), 667–675. Accessed at https://ncbi.nlm .nih.gov/pubmed/17329656 on November 7, 2017.

Vincent, E. A. (2016). *Social media as an avenue to achieving sense of belonging among college students.* American Counseling Association. Accessed at https://counseling .org/knowledge-center/vistas/by-subject2/vistas-college-students/docs/default -source/vistas/social-media-as-an-avenue on November 13, 2017.

Wenzel, A. (Ed.). (2017). *The SAGE encyclopedia of abnormal and clinical psychology.* Thousand Oaks, CA: SAGE.

Westervelt, E. (2016, September 15). *Frustration. Burnout. Attrition. It's time to address the national teacher shortage.* Accessed at www.npr.org/sections /ed/2016/09/15/493808213/frustration-burnout-attrition-its-time-to-address -the-national-teacher-shortage on July 31, 2017.

Wood, J. V., Perunovic, W. Q. E., & Lee, J. W. (2009, July 1). Positive self-statements: Power for some, peril for others [Abstract]. *Psychological Science, 20*(7). Accessed at http://journals.sagepub.com/doi/pdf/10.1111/j.1467-9280.2009.02370.x on March 5, 2018.

Your amazing brain . . . (n.d.). *Stress: Your brain and body.* Accessed at www .youramazingbrain.org/brainchanges/stressbrain.htm on December 16, 2016.

INDEX

The Beginning Teacher's Field Guide
Tina H. Boogren
The joys and pains of starting a teaching career often go undiscussed. This guide explores the personal side of teaching, offering crucial advice and support. The author details six phases every new teacher goes through and outlines classroom strategies and self-care practices.
BKF806

Supporting Beginning Teachers
Tina H. Boogren
Give new teachers the time and professional guidance they need to become expert teachers through effective mentoring. Investigate key research and examine the four types of support—physical, emotional, instructional, and institutional—that are crucial during a teacher's first year in the classroom.
BKL023

Embracing a Culture of Joy
Dean Shareski
Although fun is sometimes seen as a barrier to real learning, joy is a vital part of effective education. Discover how to equip students with the skills and qualities they'll need to achieve academic success by bringing joy to classrooms each day.
BKF730

HEART!
Timothy D. Kanold
Explore the concept of a heartprint—the distinctive impression an educator's heart leaves on students and colleagues during his or her professional career. Use this resource to reflect on your professional journey and discover how to foster productive, heart-centered classrooms and schools.
BKF749

Visit SolutionTree.com or call 800.733.6786 to order.

Wait! Your professional development journey doesn't have to end with the last pages of this book.

We realize improving student learning doesn't happen overnight. And your school or district shouldn't be left to puzzle out all the details of this process alone.

No matter where you are on the journey, we're committed to helping you get to the next stage.

Take advantage of everything from **custom workshops** to **keynote presentations** and **interactive web and video conferencing**. We can even help you develop an action plan tailored to fit your specific needs.

Let's get the conversation started.

Call 888.763.9045 today.

SolutionTree.com